A Fern Creek Press Southern Appalachian Guidebook

The Rabun County
Outdoors Companion

compiled by Brian Boyd

FERN CREEK PRESS
CLAYTON GEORGIA

The Rabun County Outdoors Companion
ISBN # 0-9625737-7-9
Published by Fern Creek Press
PO Box 1322
Clayton, GA 30525
(706) 782-5379

Copyright © 1996, 1999 Fern Creek Press

All rights reserved. No portions of this guide may be reproduced without the written permission of the publisher, excepting those portions used in conjunction with reviews for magazines or newspapers.

The author and publisher of this guidebook assume no responsibility for any loss of property, accident, injury or death sustained while visiting any of the locations described in this guidebook. Both natural and manmade changes occur which may make descriptions in this book obsolete. The very nature of the terrain and features contained here make them potentially dangerous to visit and explore. Please use caution and good common sense when in the wild.

Cover photograph: *Hawthorne's Pool, deep within rugged Tallulah Gorge - Tallulah Gorge State Park.*

Introduction

Sometimes the very best things in life are discovered when we are busy pursuing other interests - sort of like when someone meets their future spouse while on a routine trip to the grocery store. Often times life's most pleasant discoveries come quite by accident, and surely this makes a great find all the more satisfying. Such was my "discovery" of my once-future and now-present home - the ancient, enchanting mountains of Rabun County, Georgia.

Almost twenty years ago I came to Rabun County, known then to myself as that place where the movie "*Deliverance*" was filmed. You know, the film where inbred mountain men roamed the woods waiting to molest innocent outdoorsmen like myself. I seem to remember looking over my shoulder a lot that first weekend in the woods here. My first taste of Rabun County came on the Bartram and Chattooga River Trail, and like some smitten schoolboy, it was love at first sight. The sights, sounds and even smells of these mountains went straight to my head, like some sort of mountain aphrodisiac. If there was any doubt as to my intoxication, they were put to rest at my first sight of the spellbinding Chattooga River. I knew then that one day this would be my home. My courtship with this mountain country continued over the next 15 years, until in 1991 I moved my family here to experience what I perceive as "the good life."

Serenely beautiful Rabun County is truly an outdoor paradise. This is a rugged land of time-worn peaks, rolling broken ridges and picturesque hidden valleys. A land of mighty and once-mighty rivers, countless sparkling streams and majestic, dancing waterfalls. Rabun County is an enchanting land created to be explored and appreciated by anyone who loves God's creation.

Scenic Rabun County boasts many impressive natural features in a state full of superlatives. Consider a few of Rabun's natural attractions - Rabun Bald, Georgia's second highest mountain at 4,696 feet; Sky Valley, the highest valley in the state and one of the highest incorporated towns in the eastern United States. Then there's Tallulah Gorge, perhaps the most rugged gorge in the southeast with depths nearing 1,000 feet. One of Rabun's biggest attractions is the incomparable Chattooga National Wild and Scenic River, which forms Rabun's undulating eastern boundary. And this is just the beginning.

The Rabun County Outdoors Companion

Add to all this the fact that about 63% of Rabun County's 236,000+ acres are owned by the US Forest Service, and about 8% is controlled by Georgia Power and you come to one inescapable conclusion - there's plenty of forest to roam around in!

If wilderness isn't your idea of a good time, consider that Rabun is Georgia's only county to have three state parks within its borders - Tallulah Gorge State Park, Black Rock Mountain State Park, and Moccasin Creek State Park. These three members of the state park system offer three dramatically different outdoor experiences, each delightfully attractive in its own right.

Rabun County also boasts an incomparable string of sparkling, cold mountain lakes along the ancient Tallulah River. Generations of people - both locals and visitors - have been enjoying these mountain gems since the early quarter of this century. Lakes with names such as Burton, Seed, Rabun, Tallulah, and Tugalo are all popular and quite well-known around the Southeast. Activities such as boating, skiing, swimming and fishing are all top notch in this wonderful mountain playground.

Besides our splendid mountain lakes, Rabun is also quite popular for its many miles of stocked trout streams. Though you'll find most of the crowds along the popular upper Tallulah and northern portions of the Chattooga River, many more less well known yet amply stocked streams lace the county.

What else can there possibly be? Regardless of what you're looking for, if it's done in the great outdoors, it can most likely be done in Rabun County. Come on up and give Rabun County a try. You'll be glad you did. I know I was.

The Rabun County Outdoors Companion

CONTENTS

Section 1 - The State Parks

Tallulah Gorge State Park	2
North Rim Trail	5
Gorge Hiking	7
Black Rock Mountain State Park	10
Ada-Hi Falls	11
Tennessee Rock Trail	12
Edmunds Backcountry Trail	14
Moccasin Creek State Park	18

Section 2 - The Chattooga River

Russell Bridge & Vicinity	24
Sandy Ford	27
US 76 Bridge	30
Chattooga Maps	34
Chattooga River Trail	37
Lower Chattooga	41
Chattooga Floating Information	44

Section 3 - National Forest Hiking Trails

Southwest Rabun	47
Fall Branch Trail	47
Joe Branch Trail	49
Central Rabun	51
Becky Branch Falls	51
Warwoman Dell Nature Trail	52
Northwest Rabun	53
Patterson Creek Falls	53
Grassy Ridge Trail	53
Tate City	55
Coleman River Trail	56
Denton Branch Falls	57
Beech Creek Gorge	58
Appalachian Trail	61
Northeast Rabun	63
Rabun Bald	63
Holcomb Creek Trail	65
Three Forks	67
Bartram Trail	70

Section 4 - Additional Recreational Ideas

Estatoah & Mud Creek Falls	76
The Great Lakes	77
Whitewater Paddling	80
Horseback Riding	83
Trout Fishing	85
Campgrounds	87
Auto Tours	90
Emergency Numbers	92
Fern Creek Press Order Form	94

The Rabun County Outdoors Companion

About this guide...

It is quite likely that some of the descriptions included in this guidebook will become obsolete or possibly even erroneous at some point. Construction, improvements, natural disasters and even closure sometimes occur in natural areas open to visitors. If you encounter anything which you believe to be in error, please contact Fern Creek Press. We'd like to correct any misinformation for the safety and enjoyment of future visitors.

Much of the information in *The Rabun County Outdoors Companion* is quite subjective. For instance, the trail ratings used by the author may be open to various interpretations. Generally speaking, **easy** means that practically anyone can hike a particular trail, including grandma (that is, as long as grandma can get around ok). **Moderate** means that the participant should expect at least some physical exertion (couch potatoes will do some sweating, but should be alright). **Strenuous** means that you better be in pretty good physical condition or you will regret it. Also keep in mind that elevation changes are at least as important (in difficulty ratings) as mileage figures. A one-thousand foot climb may be beyond the average beginners ability. A good example of this is the hike down into Tallulah Gorge. You may not be able to discern those who fit the "out-of-shape" category by watching hikers descend into the gorge, but they become very obvious during the climb out. (They are usually draped across boulders clutching their hearts and gasping for breath.) The best advice - know *your* fitness level before attempting any unfamiliar hike. And perhaps most importantly, **never hike alone!**

Though trail maps are included in this publication, any hike into the wilderness should include Forest Service maps or US Geological Survey maps. Even with these resources there is no substitute for common sense. Many maps currently on the market contain information based on surveys completed decades ago. In other words, never completely trust one source of information. Get as many of the details as you can, and **be prepared for anything when in the outdoors**.

The Rabun County Outdoors Companion

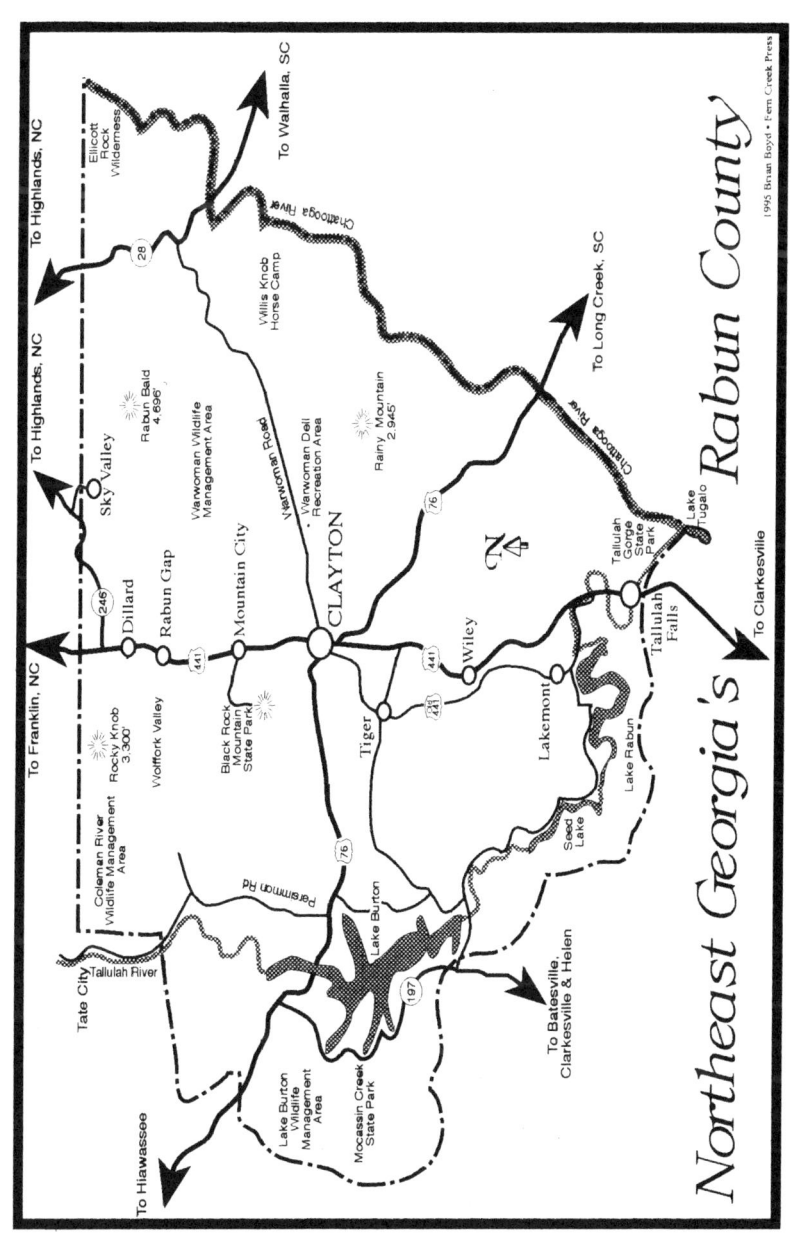

The Rabun County Outdoors Companion

The Rabun County Outdoors Companion

Section 1
Rabun County's
State Parks

Tallulah Gorge State Park

General location: Tallulah Gorge State Park is located adjacent to the town of Tallulah Falls, approximately 10 miles south of Clayton on US Hwy 441.

Additional information:

Tallulah Gorge State Park
P.O. Box 248, Tallulah Falls, GA 30573
(706) 754-7970

Jane Hurt Yarn Interpretive Center
(706) 754-7981

Terrora Campground
(706) 754-7979

Overview: Founded in 1993, Tallulah Gorge State Park is Georgia's newest edition to what already is a tremendous system of historic and scenic parks. Tallulah Gorge State Park was created by a joint venture between the Georgia Department of Natural Resources and the Georgia Power Company. The central feature of the park - obviously, is magnificent Tallulah Gorge. At nearly two miles long and almost 1,000 feet deep at its greatest point, this rugged gorge is one of the deepest in the eastern United States, and is certainly one of Georgia's greatest geological features. The park covers approximately 3,000 acres. An interpretive center and day use recreational area are among the facilities, while hiking, swimming and camping are just a few of the activities that can be enjoyed here.

The Rabun County Outdoors Companion

A Little History...

For generations vacationers to the Blue Ridge have been stopping at the overlook along old US 23/441 and gazing down into the foreboding abyss that is Tallulah Gorge. Perhaps just as popular is the main bridge spanning the upper gorge. Tourists seem to feel obligated to park their cars and stroll out onto the bridge and gaze down into the rocky chasm. Most encounters with Tallulah Gorge end here, but it was not always so, and with the establishment of Tallulah Gorge State Park, it may not be that way once again.

A visitor in the early 1950's

The Tallulah Gorge area began to attract the white man shortly after native Cherokee Indians were driven out in the early 1800's. Though still a distant 12 miles from the nearest town of Clarkesville, visitors began making the trek before the middle of the 19th century. Around this time several small "inns" began to open in the vicinity of the gorge.

The first real development in the Tallulah Gorge area began around 1870 with the opening of the Shirley Hotel, built about a mile from the gorge. This seemed to only open the floodgates, as increased interest and tourism led to a boom time for the small town of Tallulah Falls during the decade of the 1880's. The rapid development, which eventually had some 17 hotels and boarding houses in the town, was spurred in part by the advent of the Tallulah Falls Railroad, which reached the town in 1882.

A great and historical environmental fight took place in the early 1900's to save the wild Tallulah River and Tallulah Gorge from developers proposing to build a hydroelectric dam here. As everyone now knows, this battle was lost, and the Tallulah Falls dam - 116 feet high and 400 feet long across the top - was completed in 1913. With the falls in the gorge greatly diminished and the railroad line now extending all the way to Franklin, N.C., many of Tallulah's visitors now ventured farther north. The final defeat for Tallulah Falls came in December 1921, as a huge fire destroyed most of the town. The ensuing years saw most of the town's once grand inns fall into disrepair.

For years the residents of little Tallulah Falls have been looking for a way to revitalize their sagging fortunes. Perhaps with the advent of the new Tallulah Gorge State Park, something good may be in store for this historically rich town.

For an interesting and colorful description of the history of Tallulah Falls, try obtaining a copy of "The Life and Times of Tallulah...The Falls, The Gorge, The Town" by John Saye. Check locally at Tallulah Falls School for a copy.

Day Use Area

Formerly operated by Georgia Power as Terrora Park, the day use area is adjacent to lovely 63 acre Lake Tallulah. Tennis courts, a picnic area, beach, playground and hiking trails are among the features here. This area is adjacent to Hwy 441 just north of the bridge spanning the upper gorge.

Georgia Heritage Center for the Arts

Operated by the Georgia Heritage Association, this gallery features selected works from artists and craftspeople in the region. Inquire locally concerning hours of operation. Located along Hwy 441 adjacent to the Day Use Area.

Jane Hurt Yarn Interpretive Center

Centerpiece to the new park is the Jane Hurt Yarn Interpretive Center - a first-rate 16,000 square foot facility featuring classrooms, exhibits and audio visual features for visitors. Exhibits include cultural, historical, geological, natural resource and Georgia Power topics. The Interpretive Center is located along the north rim, off, appropriately, Jane Hurt Yarn Drive.

The Rabun County Outdoors Companion

Park Trails

The park currently has five hiking trails open to the public, offering a little bit of something for everyone. These trails range from the relatively easy and moderately short rim trails to strenuous, difficult hikes into Tallulah Gorge. Detailed information on each trail can be obtained at the Jane Hurt Yarn Interpretive Center. Several of the more popular trails are detailed below.

North Rim Trail
Begins at the Jane Hurt Yarn Interpretive Center
Length: 1.5 miles round trip
Difficulty: Moderate, with some inclines and stairs. Steep drop-offs - supervise children carefully!

This heavily visited trail features five outstanding overlooks of spectacular Tallulah Gorge. Follow the signs behind the interpretive center to the numbered overlooks. Overlook #1 features an excellent view into the upper gorge, and a good view downstream to Hawthorne's pool. Overlook #2 gives visitors a good look at massive Tallulah Falls dam. Gorge depth here is approximately 250 feet. Overlooks #3 and #4 peer approximately 350 feet down into Hawthorne's Pool and immediately upstream at lovely L'Eau d'or Falls. Overlook #5 provides a jaw-dropping view straight down onto massive Oceana Falls, approximately 750 feet below. This sight is the location for the remains of the north rim portion of Wallenda's cable tower. Look far downstream to glimpse Bridal Veil Falls.

L'Eau d'or (LaDore) Falls as seen during an autumn water release from the North Rim Trail.

South Rim Trail
Begins Hwy 441 bridge at Day Use Area, or from Overlook #1 along the North Rim Trail.
Length: 1.5 miles round trip
Difficulty: Moderate, with some inclines and stairs. Steep drop-offs - supervise children closely!

Recently reopened, this venerable old path has been providing visitors with breathtaking views of Tallulah Gorge's inspiring scenery for over one hundred years, though the trail was nearly destroyed by a Palm Sunday tornado in 1994. From the day use area, *carefully* cross the highway bridge and begin following the pathway.

The first overlook encountered is #6, featuring an excellent view of Hawthorne's Pool and 76 foot high Tempesta Falls. Gorge depth here is approximately 350 feet. Overlook #7 follows shortly, featuring a magnificent view of Tempesta. Gorge depth here is approximately 400 feet. Overlook #8 features a good look at Tallulah Gorge's highest major cascade, 96 foot high Hurricane Falls. Look below the overlook for the "Devil's Pulpit" rock formation, formerly a popular (and dangerous) photo spot for early gorge visitors. Overlook #9 features excellent views of mighty Hurricane Falls and massive Oceana Falls. The creek tumbling down the far side of the gorge is 600 foot high Caledonia Cascade. Gorge depth here is approximately 600 feet. Overlook #10 features yet another good view of Caledonia Cascade and high, sheer cliffs on the opposite wall of the gorge. The remains of the Wallenda tower on the North rim are visible from this overlook. The cliffs opposite this overlook are approximately 1,000 feet above the river.

Hurricane Falls Trail
By Permit Only
Begins along the South Rim Trail

This new wooden stairway was built over the bed of a long used trail accessing Hurricane Falls, and is now used extensively by boaters during whitewater releases. It also provides those in good physical condition with a more civilized means of accessing the middle gorge floor. Trail use is by permit only. Please inquire at the Jane Hurt Yarn Interpretive Center for trail specifics and regulations of use.

Stoneplace Trail
Hiking and mountain biking
By permit only
Length: 5 miles one way
Difficulty: Long, strenuous back-country trail with an overall elevation change of over 800 feet.

This newly developed trail follows a series of old roadbeds down to scenic Lake Tugalo. This trail traverses an isolated section of the park, and is generally recommended only for those accustomed to a wilderness setting. Mountain bikers will love this new addition to Tallulah Gorge State Park.
This trail is by permit only. Please inquire at the interpretive center for trail specifics.

Terrora Trail
Located in the day use area.
Length: 1 mile loop trail
Difficulty: Easy to moderate

This pathway provides a pastoral setting for a quiet walk around a finger of Tallulah Falls Lake. The trail can be accessed by the old jail just down the street from the tennis courts. The trail returns to the road (or enters the woods, depending on your direction) by the remains of the old Tallulah Falls Railroad bridge. Plans are underway to convert much of the old railroad bed into an extended trail north from this bridge. Inquire at the interpretive center for additional details.

Wallenda Cable Trail
By permit only.
Parking area located about 0.25 miles south of the Hwy 441 bridge.
Length: 1.5 miles to 3 round trip
Difficulty: Strenuous, difficult terrain, slippery conditions, numerous steep drop-offs. Not suitable for small children, (and many adults).

For decades, visitors have had unlimited access to the floor of Tallulah Gorge by this route, and countless injuries and dozens of deaths in this time attest to its danger. Now operated strictly by permit only, this trial still allows hikers to climb down into the gorge, but only in accordance with park regulations.

The Rabun County Outdoors Companion

Visitors descend approximately 0.75 mile to the river at the location of Sliding Rock (Sweet Sixteen Falls). Hikers can then work their way across the Tallulah River (access is only during low-water conditions) and head upstream to witness incredible scenery including towering cliffs, Oceana Falls and Hurricane Falls. Obtain permit and additional details at the interpretive center. Access to the gorge is restricted according to weather conditions and water releases.

Water Releases

Tallulah Gorge State Park visitors now have an added incentive to visit. During the first two weekends in April, and the first three weekends in November, special water releases (500cfs and 700 cfs) are scheduled to accomodate daredevil whitewater boaters who wish to challenge the awesome gorge. During these weekends, large crowds gather at the prime overlooks to witness these boaters plunge over waterfalls such as mighty Oceana.

Normal water flow in the gorge is 35 to 40 cfs. The park features aesthetic releases of 200 cfs during selected days in September, October and November. Call the park directly for water release dates.

Whitewater boater below Hurricane Falls.

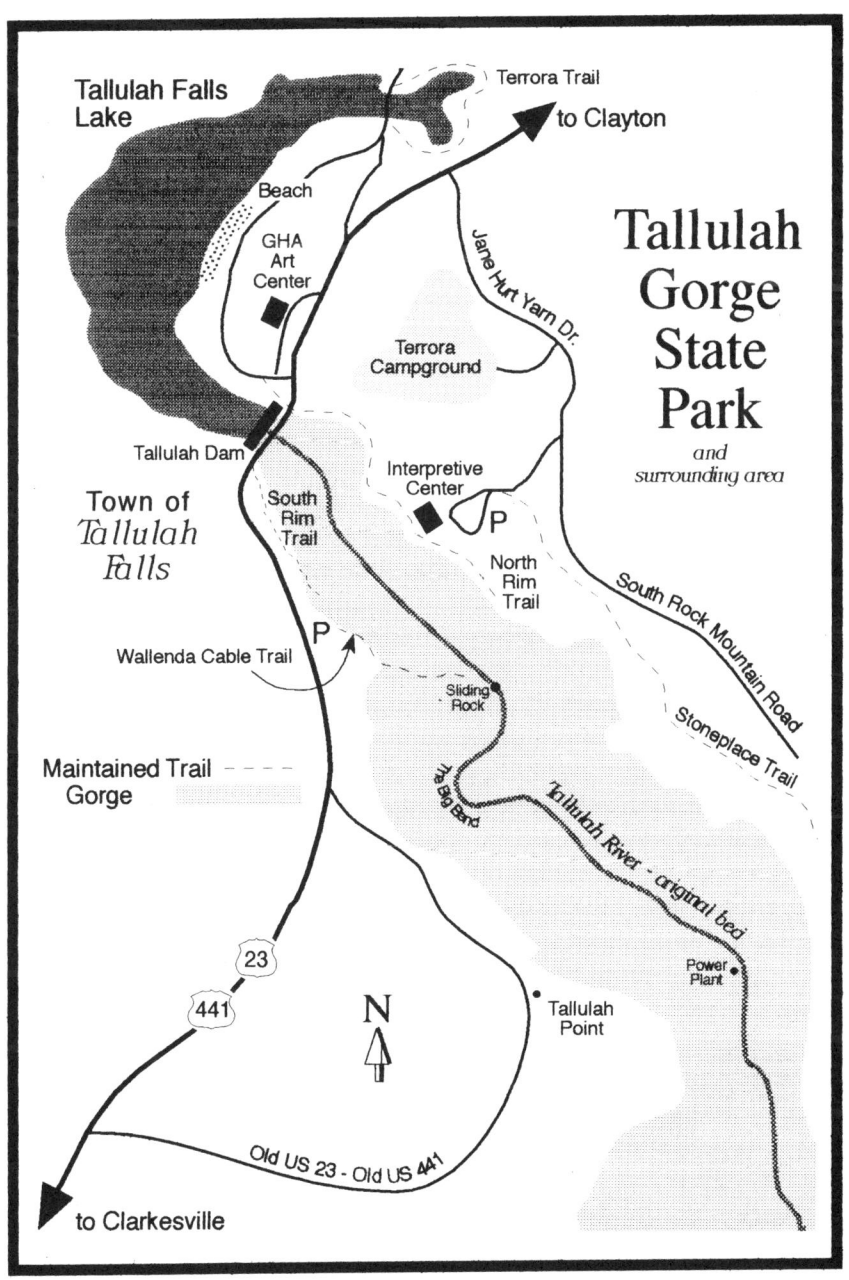

Black Rock Mountain State Park

General location: Black Rock Mountain State Park is located approximately 3 miles north of Clayton off Hwy 441 in Mountain City.

Additional information:
Black Rock Mountain State Park
P.O. Drawer A
Mountain City, GA 30562
(706) 746-2141

Visitor Center Hours
8:00 a.m. - 5:00 p.m. daily

Park Emergency Phone
(706) 746-2818

Overview: Black Rock Mountain State Park, known for its smooth, sheer cliffs of dark granite, has its claim to fame in the fact that it is Georgia's highest state park. This spectacularly scenic 1,803 acre park contains six peaks that reach above the lofty 3,000 foot level, offering enchanting views of the Southern Blue Ridge.

    The park's visitor center gazes down over sheer southern cliffs almost 2,000 feet onto the picturesque town of Clayton and well beyond into the foothills and piedmont region of South Carolina. Here along the backbone of the park's main peak you'll find a delightful, shady picnic area and pleasant playground for the kids.

    For a park that sits astride a series of rugged peaks, there sure are a lot of facilities to enjoy. Black Rock Mountain State Park features 52 tent and trailer campsites, 11 walk-in campsites, 10 rental cottages, a pioneer camping area and a backcountry camping area.

The Rabun County Outdoors Companion

Black Rock Mountain State Park also features something you wouldn't normally expect to find in a park which sits astride a series of mountains - namely a 17 acre fishing lake. This popular attraction is stocked with bass, bream, catfish and trout.

And don't forget Black Rock's trail system, which is second to none among Georgia's parks. Ten miles of delightfully different pathways take visitors to some of the park's best sites, most within a stone's throw of the Eastern Continental Divide.

Sounds like it has a bit of everything, right? And remember - the one thing you'll never run out of here is scenery, with an assortment and abundance of yawning mountain vistas. Do yourself a big favor - next time you're motoring up Hwy 441 toward some other mountain destination, take a little detour up to Black Rock Mountain State Park. You'll be glad you did.

Note: don't forget that Georgia's State Parks require a valid ParkPass for entry.

The Black Rock Mountain State Park Trails

Ada-Hi Falls Trail

Overview: This short but steep trail leads to a tiny, trickling cascade.
Trail Length: 0.2 mile one way
Difficulty: moderate - due to 200 foot descent.
Hazards: watch for possible slippery steps!

Ada-Hi is Cherokee for "forest", though I must admit I thought it was more correctly translated "tiny trickles" the first time I visited here. The Ada-Hi Falls Trail is a short plunge down into a steep ravine that shrouds tiny Taylor Creek. Here, just a few hundred yards below its headspring, this miniscule branch softly flows across the face of a high rock wall. A small observation platform allows you to enjoy the falls and pool your energy for the burst required to get back up to the trailhead. Although the falls can virtually disappear during a prolonged dry spell, the hike is nonetheless worthy for its short journey into the dense forest of rhododendron and mixed hardwoods. Keep a sharp eye out for a wide variety of wildflowers which bloom all across the park throughout the warm seasons.

To reach the Ada-Hi Falls trailhead, proceed to the Trading Post near the main campground. The campground is located just off the main park road near the Cowee Overlook.

The Tennessee Rock Trail

Overview: Great loop trail featuring diverse forests and excellent views!
Trail Length: 2.2 miles
Difficulty: Moderate - over 300 foot elevation gain.
Hazards: Trail passes several dangerous cliffs.

Now *this* is a trail for people who like a little diversity with their hike! The Tennesse Rock Trail is a thoroughly enjoyable 2.2 mile loop which passes through a wide variety of forest environments along the way to conquering the 3,640 foot crown of Black Rock Mountain. The path alternates between a cool, moist northern cove and the high, relatively dry ridgetop. Make sure you purchase a copy of the park's interpretive guide to this trail - it is a delightful companion guaranteed to make your hike here more enjoyable.

From the parking area, the Tennessee Rock Trail follows yellow blazes as it enters the woods heading towards a nearby fork. Follow the path to the right and proceed into the cool mixed hardwood forest of oak, poplar and hickory. The pathway here is mostly level and quite pleasant to walk. A prolific variety of beautiful ferns, mosses and seasonal wildflowers are a feast to the senses. Among the most popular of the wildflowers to be found here are several varieties of lovely trilliums.

Almost halfway into the 2+ mile journey, the trail enters a fragrant grove of pristine white pines. This is a good place to pause, as the path soon turns eastward and begins a steep, switchbacking ascent up the mountain's western flank. All your sweating and heavy breathing has its rewards though, as once you attain the ridgeline the path features grand scenery.

The Rabun County Outdoors Companion

The absolute highlight of the hike comes along the ridgetop, several hundred yards past the actual highpoint of the mountain (3,640'). Here on the northwestern slope of the summit is the popular Tennessee Rock Overlook, featuring one of Georgia's grandest mountain panoramas. The actual elevation here is 3,625', though the 15 foot drop from the summit does nothing to diminish the view. A truly inspiring scene unfolds before you as a seemingly endless string of mountain peaks receed into the far horizon. As with other overlooks, a topo map or forest service map will help you identify the visible peaks.

To the far left you may be lucky enough to spot Brasstown Bald, Georgia's highest mountain. Look for the observation tower, visible even from nearly 30 miles. Below and to the right is scenic Wolffork Valley, completely surrounded by the rugged, densely forested summits. This undeveloped overlook, set among gnarled rhododendrons and greyish boulders, is truly a spot to savor.

Beyond Tennessee Rock, the trail continues along the Eastern Continental Divide. This is a great spot to teach a little geography to the kids. Try telling them that while spitting (they may suggest other bodily functions) to the left goes to the Gulf of Mexico, spitting to the right goes to the Atlantic. Even some adults seem to have trouble with this concept. By the way, the view to the south offers glimpses of nearby Clayton and the lower ridges and peaks to the south.

The trail descends rather quickly after coming in contact with the main park road (often used as a shortcut to Tennessee Rock by the lazy and undedicated), switching down the north side of Black Rock again through a mature hardwood forest. The pathway soon intersects the original trail fork and brings you back to the trailhead parking area.

The trailhead parking area lies along the main road to the park's visitor center between the Cowee Overlook and the Blue Ridge Overlook. The area is well-marked and features several convenient picnic tables.

The Rabun County Outdoors Companion

James E. Edmonds Backcountry Trail

Overview: Excellent day hike featuring scenic vistas and ever-changing forests.
Trail Length: 7.2 miles
Difficulty: Moderate to Strenuous
Hazards: Sheer cliffs around several overlooks and careless motorists at road crossings.

The James Edmonds Backcountry Trail is appropriately named. This is no city-slicker path. One of Black Rock's staff once told me of an overconfident tourist boasting that he could do this trail in just a few hours. About 5 hours later, an exhausted hiker, several pounds lighter, made his way back to the trailhead. The trail elevations range from around 2,240' near Black Rock Lake to near 3,300' at the trailhead, so expect a great deal of up-and-down hiking. In fact, you may think you've been on nature's roller coaster by the time you return to the trailhead.

The path shares starting points with the Tennessee Rock Trail. Make sure you follow the signs, and perhaps more importantly, make sure you are following **orange** blazes. If not, you're sure to think you've covered this trail in record time. You might also think that this guide is more than a little off in its general descriptions.

The initial 0.7 mile descends gently to a trail fork. Follow the path to the right, traversing the loop in a counter-clockwise direction. The trail gently undulates along an old roadbed and generally wide path through alternating patches of rhododendron and hardwoods. The path drops down onto North Germany Road at mile 1.4. Beyond - another prolonged descent brings you to a crossing of noisy Taylor Creek at mile 2.5.

For hard-core hikers, the real fun starts here, as the next half mile features an exhilarating 600 foot climb to rugged Scruggs Knob (elevation 3,048'). The area atop Scruggs features an eerily impressive grove of twisted mountain laurel. Beyond, the trail follows an old roadbed for 0.5 mile to Gibson Gap and a trail junction at mile 3.5. To the right is the Lookoff Mountain Spur Trail. To the left the main trail continues.

The 0.7 mile spur trail to Lookoff is well worth the effort, even if you're not headed to the backcountry camping area. This path follows an old roadbed uphill to Lookoff Mountain (elevation 3,162'), the northernmost of the park's peaks. The area features several excellent overlooks to the north, all perched along sheer granite cliffs. A rugged backcountry camping area is nestled closeby - just perfect for an easy 2 day trip. (Special note: you better have a permit before camping here!) The views from Lookoff feature a picturesque expanse of the valley encompassing the headwaters of the Little Tennessee River. This area is also the sight of filming for a few "B" movies over the years.

Back along the main trail, the path descends from the Lookoff Mountain junction and proceeds one mile down to the crossing of Taylor's Chapel Road at mile 4.5. This crossing occurs near the head of scenic 17 acre Black Rock Lake, providing a good resting point before the final return ascent to the trailhead begins. Just beyond the road crossing, the trail passes over Taylor's Creek and skirts near the southern shoreline of the lake.

Greasy Creek (yuck!) is soon encountered and crossed, the trail roughly following the tumbling stream through thick rhododendrons before a second footbridge crossing and a 0.4 mile uphill climb to the original trail fork. The final 0.7 mile climbs about 700 vertical feet back up to the trailhead. Congratulations - you've earned a rest!

Follow directions to the Tennessee Rock Trailhead. To walk only portions of the trail, refer to the official park maps to plan your routes.

The Rabun County Outdoors Companion

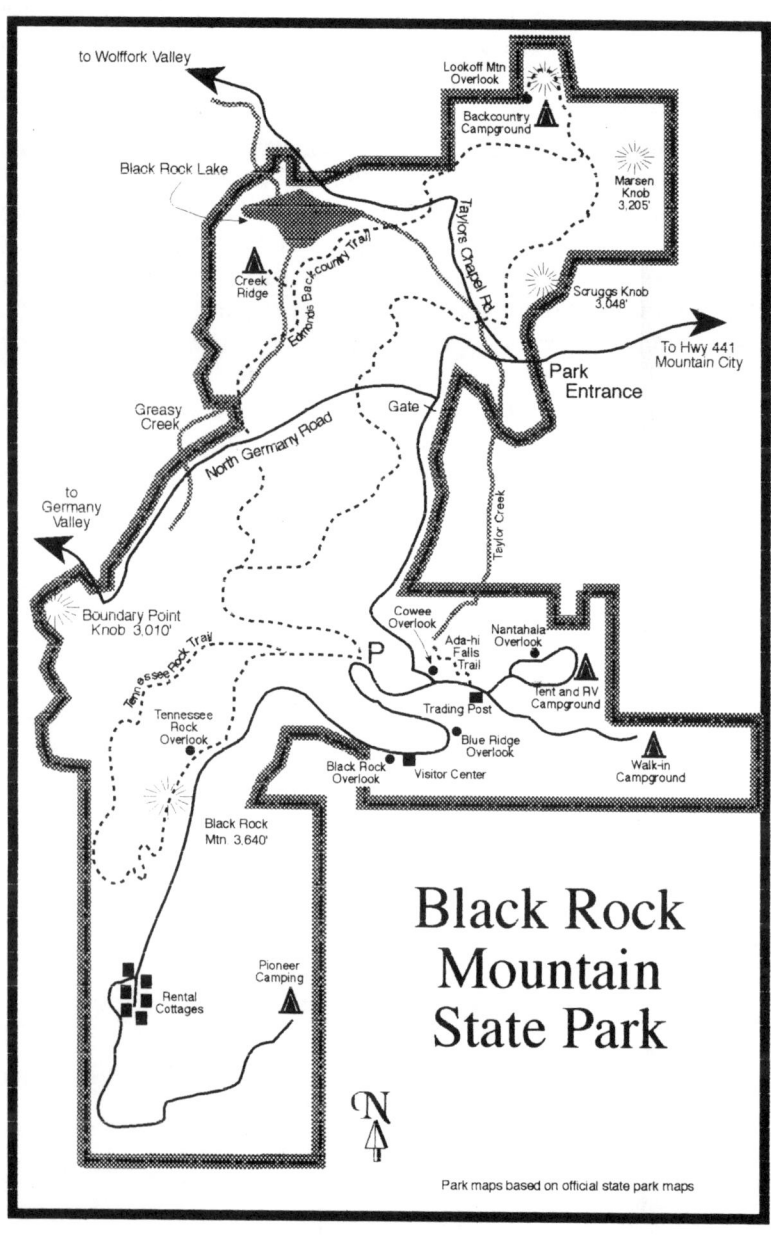

*The magnificent view from the Black Rock Overlook
Photo by Anthony Lampros*

*Early morning fog from the Cowee Overlook.
Photo by Anthony Lampros*

Moccasin Creek State Park

General location: Moccasin Creek State Park is located on the northwestern shore of Lake Burton on Hwy 197, about 20 miles north of Clarkesville and about 16 miles west of Clayton.

Additional information:
Moccasin Creek State Park
Rt. #1, Box 1634
Clarkesville, GA 30523
(706) 947-3194

Park Hours
7:00 a.m. - 10:00 p.m. daily

Park Office Hours
8:00 a.m. - 5:00 p.m.

Park Emergency Phone
(706) 947-3710 or 947-3016

Overview: Scenic Moccasin Creek State Park lies nestled along the northwestern shore of beautiful Lake Burton, and provides visitors with a wide variety of recreational opportunities. Though the park itself is only 32 acres, 2,800 acre Lake Burton and the surrounding Forest Service land provide some great hiking, boating, and fishing.

Campers will love Moccasin Creek's 54 tent and trailer campsites. For one thing, all the campsites are relatively close to the cool, 1866' elevation lake. For another, the campground isn't so large that you lose some sort of a sense of community (plus close proximity to the necessary facilities).

The park's facilities include a picnic area and open-air pavilion along Lake Burton. There is a fishing pier for handicapped visitors along with a playground and recreational area for various sports.

Boating - As you might well expect, boating is one of the main features of Moccasin Creek. Lake Burton is a worthy destination both for pleasure boating or fishing. A public boat ramp is available at the fish hatchery next to the park, and a private boat dock is available for registered campers within the park. Those wishing to rent boats should check at nearby LaPrade's Marina, located on Hwy 197 about two miles south of the park.

Fishing - Moccasin Creek, strategically located between the park and the fish hatchery, can be fished by children 11 and younger and by persons with an honorary license. Trout fishing for the public is good along the section of Moccasin Creek above the park.

Lake Burton Fish Hatchery - Located next-door to the park, this state owned facility raises rainbow trout to be stocked in numerous lakes and streams across North Georgia. Children in particular love to observe the tens of thousands of small trout as they move in unison through the long "raceway" tanks. Hatchery hours are 8:00 a.m. to 4:30 p.m. daily.

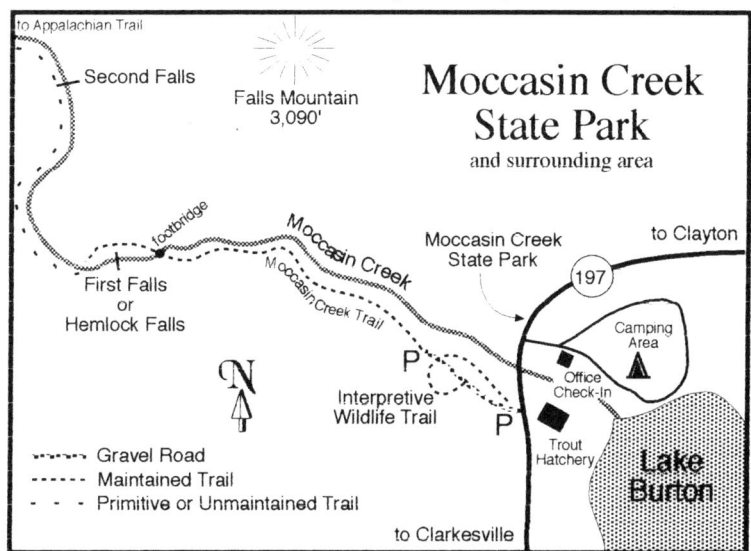

The Rabun County Outdoors Companion

Moccasin Creek State Park Trails

Nature Trail

Overview: A short, pleasant stroll through a woodland setting.
Trail Length: 1.2 mile loop
Difficulty: easy
Hazards: none

Alongside noisy Moccasin Creek, a delightful 1.2 mile nature trail loops through the surrounding forest. While there is nothing dramatic here, it does provide a good backdrop for a pleasant stroll. Seniors and parents with small children may particularly enjoy this walk. There are numerous spots alongside the creek where visitors can relax and enjoy nature's serenade.

The trailhead for this pathway is across the highway from the park at the trout hatchery intake.

Hemlock Falls Trail (a.k.a. Moccasin Creek Trail)

Overview: A very scenic trail featuring scenic Moccasin Creek and several waterfalls.
Trail Length from trailhead:
        1.5 miles one way to 1st falls (maintained)
        2.0 miles to 2nd falls (unmaintained)
Difficulty: moderate
Hazards: those continuing above the first falls must make a hazardous stream crossing. Trail to 2nd falls is rough and several slides have made the trail difficult to negotiate. Area around 2nd falls is very slippery.

One of Rabun County's most beautiful hikes closely follows tumbling Moccasin Creek for 2.0 scenic miles and features two sparkling cascades. Although largely unmaintained above the first falls, this popular trail attracts large numbers of hikers because of its proximity to the park. Although several guidebooks describe this trail as reaching up to the Appalachian Trail at Addis Gap, beyond 2.0 miles the trail is in very poor condition and hikers should be advised against attempting it.

The Rabun County Outdoors Companion

Due to the present condition of much of the trail, only the first 2 miles up to the 2nd falls will be described.

The initial 0.5 mile is along a gravel road and may be driven if desired (all mileage figures here include the dirt road as part of the trail). A broad clearing at the end of the road may be used as a parking area. The trail continues beyond several vehicle-blocking mounds, enters the national forest and continues along the abandoned roadbed upstream, closely paralleling the rushing creek.

At approximately 1.25 miles, the path crosses Moccasin Creek via a newly built wooden footbridge. Be thankful for this newest convenience, as previous visitors were forced to cross the creek on a slippery fallen log with only a suspended guy wire to steady them.

Just beyond the footbridge, a scenic 15-foot waterfall crashes over a rocky ledge into a lovely, green pool. While many refer to this cascade as First Falls, park literature refers to it as Hemlock Falls, and visitors will find this name somewhat obvious. The pool is bordered by a relatively flat open area, providing easy access to both the pool and falls. Swimmers often fill the pool in the hot summertime to enjoy the icy waters of Moccasin Creek.

Above Hemlock Falls, the trail crosses again to the left bank, though without the benefit of a footbridge. Hikers must rock-hop or wade across the shallow stream before continuing up the now rough and narrow path to the 2nd upper falls. Several slides and washouts have made this trail pretty tough to enjoy, though the upper falls is worth the effort. At about mile 2.0 the falls come into view. This 25-foot cascade spills over a steep ledge into a small pool via two distinct tongues. Steep banks and slippery rocks choke the pool, making for difficult and dangerous viewing. Use extreme caution here!

Note: Unless you are an experienced hiker travelling in a small group, it would be wise to avoid the hike to the upper falls. The trail has historically been in pretty bad shape.

This path shares the same trailhead as the nature trail.

Section 2
Rabun County's
Chattooga River Country

The Chattooga River

The magnificent and majestic Chattooga River forms the entire eastern boundary of Georgia's Rabun County - nearly 40 river miles in all. The river contains some of the wildest whitewater in the eastern part of the U.S., attracting thousands each year to Rabun County and the surrounding area. The river became instantly famous as the primary location for the filming of the whitewater drama "*Deliverance*". While the whitewater may be the main draw here, the hiking and camping opportunities are also outstanding. The Chattooga remains one of the Southeast's last free-flowing rivers, and offers those with a love of the outdoors a true wilderness experience.

In 1968, Congress passed the National Wild and Scenic Rivers Act, aimed at preserving many of our nation's most spectacular waterways. Under this act, a river must contain characteristics of the following:

1) **Wild** - unpolluted, undammed, with primitive surroundings - accessible only by foot.
2) **Scenic** - undammed, with undeveloped shoreline, and accessible by road.
3) **Recreational** - easily accessible by road, with some development and pre-existing dams ok.

On May 10, 1974, Congress designated the Chattooga River a member of the National Wild and Scenic River System. Of the river's entire 57 miles, 40 are classified as "Wild", 2 miles are "Scenic" and 15 miles are listed as "Recreational". However you want to classify it, this is one great river.

This guidebook will primarily describe the trails along the river, but will also give a brief, general description of the portions of the river open to boating. For more information on the Chattooga, obtain a Forest Service river map and a copy of "*The Chattooga Wild and Scenic River*" by Fern Creek Press.

The Russell Bridge Area

General location: The Russell Bridge/Hwy 28 crossing is located about 20 driving miles northeast of Clayton.

Overview: Scenic Highway 28 crosses the Chattooga River along a relatively calm section of this famed river. In fact, for a number of miles in either direction, the river never raises its voice beyond relatively tame shoals and small ledges. An abundance of trails and footpaths - among them the famous Bartram and Chattooga River Trails - combine to create a real paradise for hikers and fishermen. There are special sections in this book which deal with the Bartram and Chattooga River Trails in their Rabun County entirety.

The area around Russell Bridge begs to be explored on foot. A veritable maze of old roads and trails run alongside or near the river, most eventually reaching some "special" area of some sort or another.

Within a mile or so of the bridge you can choose to go in any direction. **To the south**, the combined Bartram and Chattooga River Trail meanders along the high riverbank through a peaceful valley. The trail itself continues almost 20 miles down to US 76 east of Clayton, but dayhiking in the vicinity of the bridge is very worthwhile. Just 0.25 mile south of the bridge, the trail turns north briefly before fording the West Fork Chattooga River just below Big Slide, a tumbling river-wide shoal.

To the north, the combined trails head away from Russell bridge on the South Carolina side, and offer easy to moderate hiking for 3.5 miles up to several small waterfalls at Lick Log Creek. Besides these well-known pathways, there is one other area you may want to explore - Reed Creek.

Reed Creek Bottoms and Gorge

Overview: Excellent day hike featuring sparkling Chattooga River and scenic Reed Creek.
Trail Length: various combinations, though 4 - 5 miles round trip would be very common.
Difficulty: Easy to moderate. Reed Creek Gorge - strenuous.
Hazards: Limbs and heavy undergrowth in spots. Slippery rocks in Reed Creek Gorge.

Often times the main trails tend to get a little congested, even out in the "wilderness". One good option for those wishing to explore in the Russell Bridge vicinity is to plan a day hike into the Reed Creek watershed.

Several hundred yards north of the bridge, an old logging road -now gated - winds back through the hills before coming alongside the Chattooga at about mile 1.2. This old roadbed not only provides a shortcut around an extended bend in the river, but also provides a very easy, enjoyable hike through a predominantly white pine forest.

Once back alongside the river, the path narrows somewhat as it runs about 15 feet above the water along steep slopes. Look out for several earth slides which have taken a great deal of the trail down into the riverbed.

At about mile 1.7 the trail enters the broad, flat flood plain (also known as a "bottom") of Reed Creek. Much of this area consists of an old field planted in loblolly pine years ago. While the area close to the river is still somewhat open - though overgrown with tall grasses - the bottoms up Reed Creek are quite thick in white pine and heavily shaded.

Noisy Reed Creek, a fairly substantial stream averaging 15 to 20 feet wide, flows along the eastern flank of the bottoms and enters the Chattooga along a wide, placid stretch. Several old trails cut through heavy underbrush and head north before shortly converging in the white pine stand and following an old roadbed up to the mouth of steep Reed Creek Gorge.

From this point on, there isn't much of a real trail to follow, but anyone with backcountry hiking experience can explore the gorge if they use caution. Numerous high shoals and small waterfalls can be found interspersed along the steep, rocky creek. Several publications and maps list a high falls a mile or so up the gorge, but reaching this would take a good bit of effort. This is a wild area - take care here. A recent visit suggests that some of the old trails are being reconstructed or improved - perhaps in the near future the area will be more user-friendly.

Back at the river, hikers can explore downstream toward Russell Bridge. An old roadbed - now pretty well choked with rhododendron and underbrush - runs downstream alongside the river, providing access to several hospitable sandy beaches and deep, emerald green pools. Heading southward from Reed Creek Bottoms, pick up this riverside trail by veering to the left across a wildlife clearing and eventually following the roadbed back into the woods after several hundred yards.

If you follow this route back to the bridge- almost 2 miles by river - be sure to follow the roadbed (more like a path) as it angles away from the river and hugs the western slopes of Brack Hill. The undergrowth alongside the river anywhere near Russell Bridge is very heavy and not worth trying to negotiate - unless you like cuts, scratches and wicked thorns. While several publications list a path here, it is long ago overgrown.

Of special note back at the bridge is the beaver dam behind the parking area just west of the bridge. Several ponds are clearly visible in this old field- now a wide, open marsh.

To reach Russell Bridge from Clayton, follow Warwoman Road for about 14 miles. At the stop sign, turn right onto Hwy 28 and proceed south for several miles to the parking area on the left just before the bridge.

The Sandy Ford Area

General location: The Sandy Ford area of the Chattooga lies almost 10 miles due east of Clayton.

Overview: Sandy Ford features a nice, wide beach and extended pool along the scenic Chattooga River. The Bartram and Chattooga River Trails wind through the area, and a short spur trail upstream of the ford leads out to Dick's Creek Falls.

Sandy Ford is a beautiful pooled area along the Chattooga located about 3 miles south of Earl's Ford, the major launching point for Section 3 boaters. The South Carolina side of Sandy Ford is an alternate put-in point, but the Rabun County side also offers some excellent recreational opportunities. This immediate area features hiking, camping, fishing and swimming opportunities. The area is also a popular spot for locals, as this is one of the few spots on the river where visitors can still drive their vehicles to the river's edge.

The Georgia side features a nice sandy beach - hence the name. The river here is fairly slow and quite wide - just right for swimming or wading. Just upstream from the beach and pool, the final drops of the Stairsteps - a Class 3 rapid - can be glimpsed. Two small islands split the river here, with mammoth grey rocks jutting from the riverbed.

Both the Chattooga River Trail and the Bartram Trail can be accessed within a half-mile of the river, making numerous day-hikes possible.

From Clayton, drive east on Warwoman Road for 5.4 miles to Sandy Ford Road on the right. Follow for 0.65 mile to a low water bridge on the left which crosses Warwoman Creek. Turn here and proceed 4 miles to where the road fords Dick's Creek for the second time. The road beyond this point is often in very poor condition - you may choose to either park here and walk the remaining distance (less than one mile) or risk driving across the tricky creek and on down to the river along an old roadbed that seems to defy improvement. One hint: it could take a while to get a tow truck here.

Dick's Creek Falls Spur Trail

Overview: Excellent day hike featuring sparkling Chattooga River and scenic Dick's Creek Falls
Trail Length: various combinations. 0.5 mile one way is the shortest route possible.
Difficulty: Easy
Hazards: Steep dropoffs around the falls. A few tricky junctions near the waterfall.

Dick's Creek Falls slides into the majestic Chattooga River over an unusually smooth 50 foot cleft of exposed granite. One of the grandest things about this waterfall is the fact that it is offset by the pounding whitewater of Dick's Creek Ledge, a major class 4 rapid just a few hundred feet away. Boaters have always known about this scenic waterfall, yet hikers will find this stroll quite easy. This cascade is also known as "Five Finger Falls", and one trip will tell you exactly why. It is a widely held opinion that the view from the top of the waterfall is one of the wildest in the southern mountains!

Following the directions to Sandy Ford, proceed to the second ford of Dick's Creek. Park here and walk downstream along the creek to the falls. An alternate route would be to proceed across the ford uphill for several hundred yards to the Bartram Trail crossing - marked by a large inscribed boulder. From here turn north and proceed 0.5 mile to the spur trail on the right which follows Dick's Creek downstream to the falls.

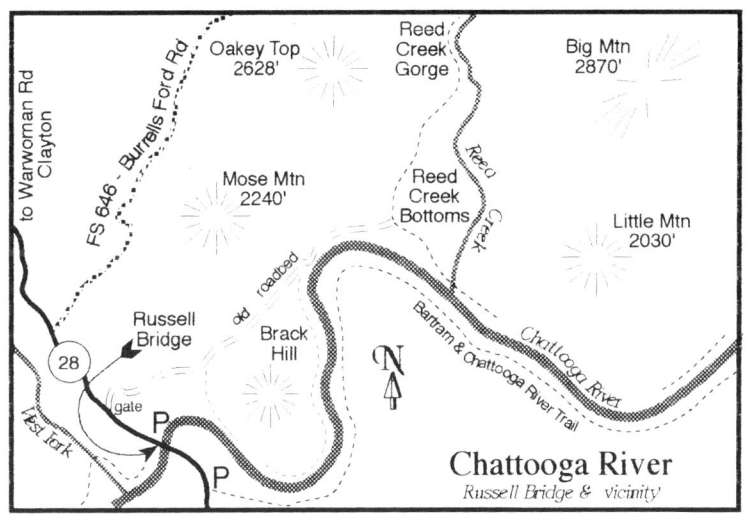

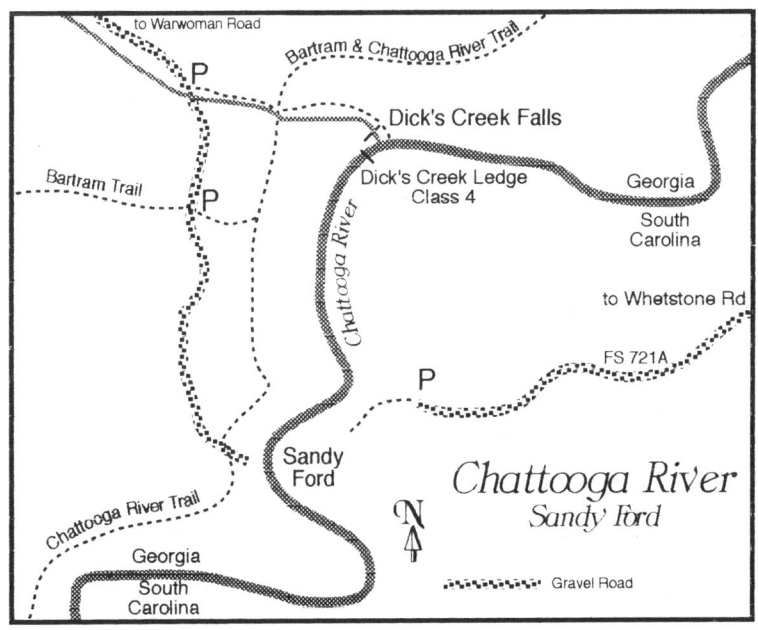

The 76 Bridge Area

General location: The US 76 Chattooga River bridge is located 9 miles southeast of Clayton.

Overview: US Highway 76 crosses the Chattooga River just downstream from a major class 5 rapid - Bull Sluice. Besides the whitewater - a wide, sandy beach beckons visitors to come and enjoy the river at its most accessible point.

M any a visitor has looked upon the Chattooga for the very first time at the US 76 bridge. Wide and shallow with only a few small shoals in sight, perhaps motorists think that the entire river is as tame as the stretch within sight of the bridge. One of the great things about the US 76 access is that it doesn't take long to prove this reasoning wrong. All one has to do is walk upstream for several hundred yards and the Chattooga will reveal its nasty side at the rugged class 5 rapid Bull Sluice.

Trails head up the riverbanks on both the Georgia and South Carolina side. The path on the South Carolina bank is both shorter and easier, but the Georgia path offers a more "intimate" view of the rapid. Take your pick - you're sure to enjoy either one. The long and winding Chattooga River Trail ends here at the bridge - but only for now. Plans are in the works which could extend this exciting trail south from the bridge, eventually linking up with a trail system now being developed at the newly created Tallulah Gorge State Park. Also worth mentioning here are the remains of the old 76 bridge, still spanning the river.

A large, paved parking area lies just across the bridge on the South Carolina side of the river. Most boaters floating Sections 3 & 4 use this lot, as it features a paved path down to the water, making carrying a loaded canoe, kayak or raft somewhat easier. The only facilities here currently are toilets and trash containers. Several informational boards are displayed near the restroom area.

Bull Sluice Trails

Overview: Great short hikes to the powerful class 5 rapid.
Trail Length: several hundred yards.
Difficulty: SC trail - easy. GA trail - moderate
Hazards: Steep trail slopes and very slippery rocks around the river. Dangerous currents around Bull Sluice.

If you are considering running the Chattooga River and want to see a little of it from terra firma first, you may want to make a stop at the 76 bridge and take a little walk up to see Bull Sluice. The easiest and shortest way to view this rapid originates at the South Carolina parking area.

Follow the paved trail downhill toward the river, then follow the gravel spur trail north for a few hundred yards. This path ends on a rock outcropping well above the river which offers a bird's eye view of the madness below. Here, the mighty Sluice falls a total of about 15 feet through a series of entrance rapids and a two-tiered toilet bowl of a drop.

Foolish first time visitors sometimes downplay the extent of the drop, but rest assured - it looks a lot different from your tiny little boat as you race through the rapid. Spend some time here during the warm season and you're sure to see some great wipe-outs.

Another short trail -this one more difficult - runs about 0.4 mile up the Georgia bank to the Sluice. Follow the Chattooga River Trail for several hundred yards, then take the first right fork. This path immediately begins a gentle descent down to the riverbank. You may have to do a little scrambling over the many downed trees which floodwaters wash onshore. The trail passes one particularly interesting overhanging rockface along the way. After a rock-hopping crossing of Pole Creek, any number of routes takes you atop the huge outcropping which creates Bull Sluice.

Visitors on the Georgia side can look straight down into the violent double drop as boaters pass within a few yards of spectators. This is a great place for action photos, but watch your step and your children, as this can be a treacherous spot.

From Clayton, take US 76 east and follow for 8 miles to the bridge. There is a small parking area on the Georgia side and a large parking area with restrooms on the South Carolina side.

The Rabun County Outdoors Companion

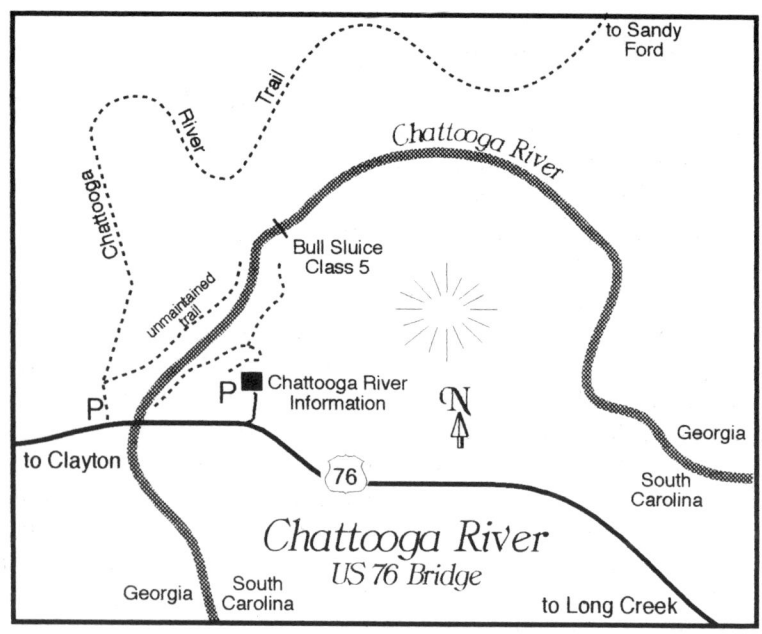

Preparing to drop into Class V Bull Sluice - Section 3

The Rabun County Outdoors Companion

Dick's Creek Ledge and the Chattooga River from the brink of Dick's Creek Falls - Section 3

The Rabun County Outdoors Companion

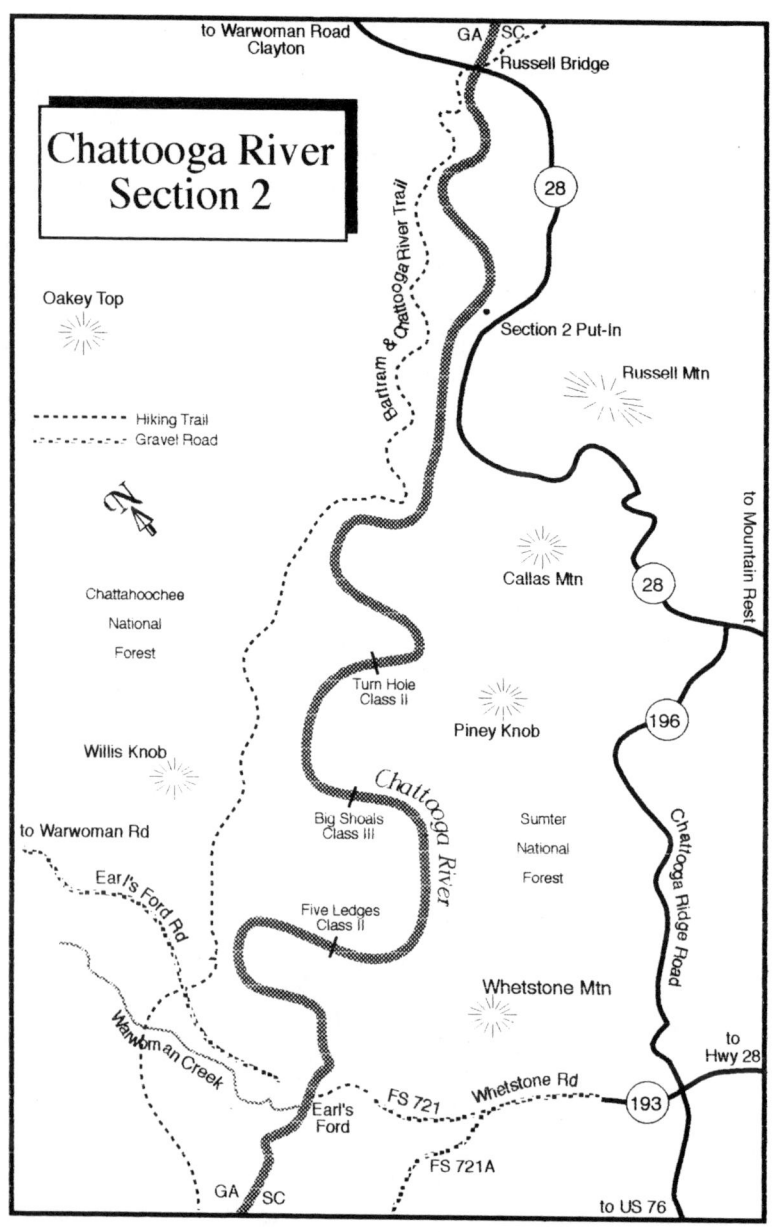

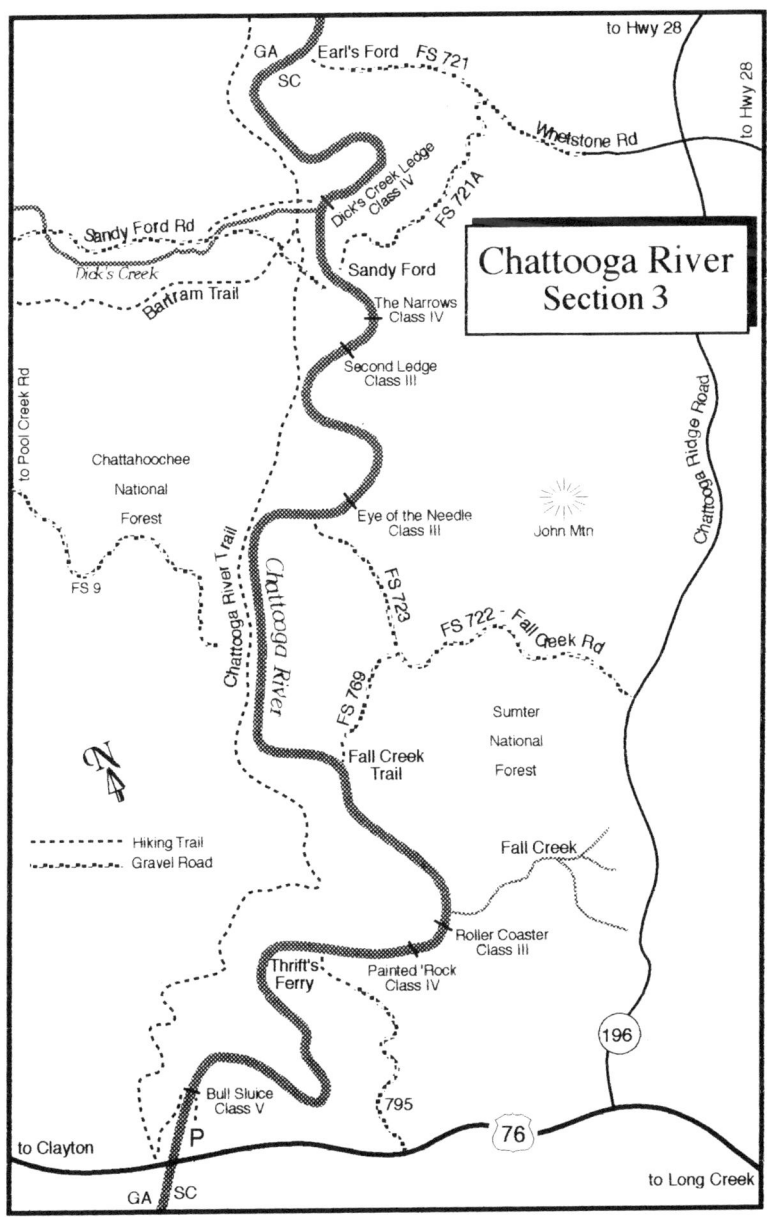

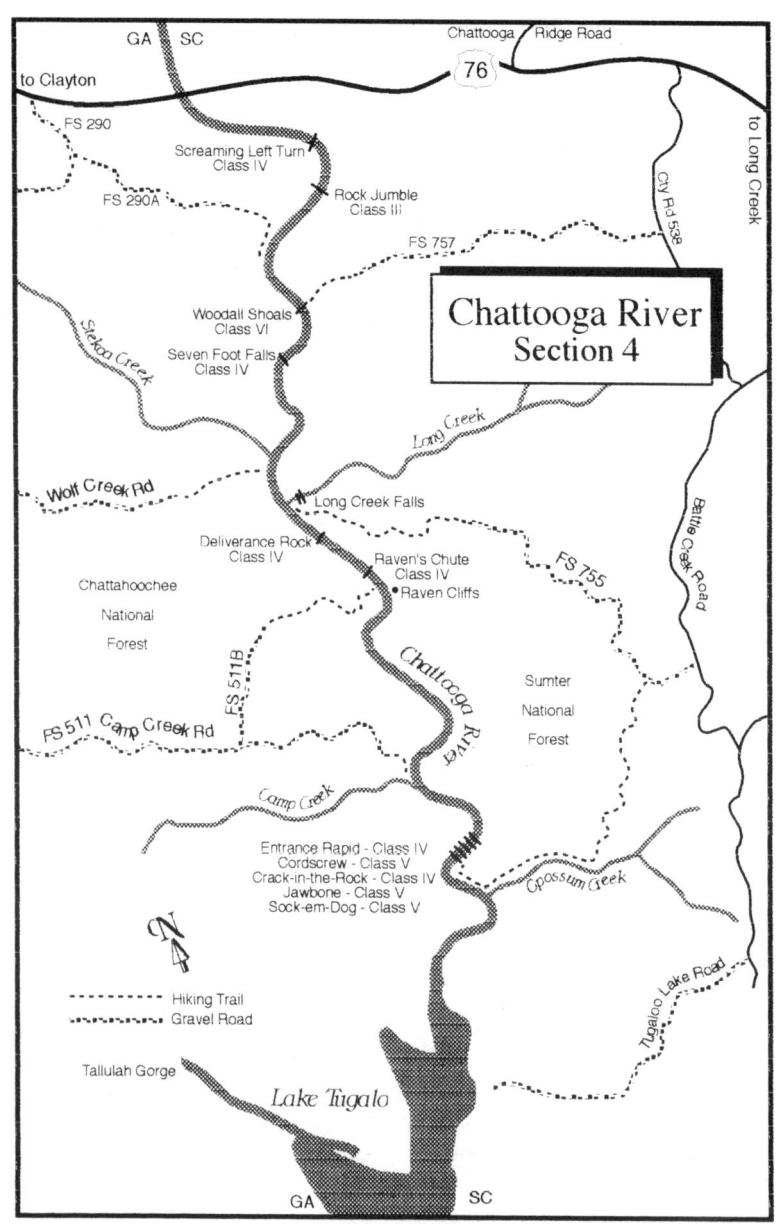

The Chattooga River Trail

General location: Rabun County's portion of the Chattooga River Trail roughly follows the course of the Chattooga, and generally lies about 10 - 12 miles east to northeast of Clayton.

Overview: This is a beautiful wilderness trail, though it may not be exactly what one would expect. Only a limited portion of the trail actually runs alongside the river. The remainder winds through the protected river corridor, normally within a quarter-mile of the Chattooga. Nevertheless, Rabun's portion of this popular pathway offers several excellent opportunities for both dayhikes and overnight trips.

Russell Bridge to Sandy Ford

Overview: Excellent day hike featuring sparkling Chattooga River, Dick's Creek Falls and numerous camping spots. Trail is described north to south.
Trail Length: 9.8 miles
Difficulty: Easy to moderate

From the Highway 28 crossing at Russell Bridge, it is an enchanting 10 mile walk south down to the Bartram and Chattooga River Trail split just west of Sandy Ford. This portion of the pathway runs along the segment of river known as Section 2, with the trail rating no higher than moderate in difficulty. Overall elevation changes are minimal, but some confusion can result due to numerous fishing paths along the river. The official trail is marked with a white diamond. Since this portion of the path combines with the Bartram Trail, a rectangular yellow blaze is also present. As always, carry a good set of maps to be sure.

Heading southwest from the Highway 28 bridge the trail winds sidewalk flat for about 0.25 mile before turning north and following the West Fork of the Chattooga upstream to a wet ford. The crossing can be a little deeper than you might like during wet weather. **Use caution anytime you ford a stream, and stay out of the water when it's high!** This particular crossing occurs only yards downstream of Big Slide, one of Section 2's lively class II rapids.

The next three miles closely follow the river, often within easy view of the sparkling clear waters. The trail passes through a developing forest, with wintertime views of the valley - known as Long Bottom Ford - which are truly enchanting.

The valley narrows dramatically at the southern end, with the trail turning sharply right and crossing a small bridge over Adline Branch. The next 2 miles are moderately strenuous, with the trail alternately climbing and descending well back from the river. The Laurel Branch crossing announces a series of twisting turns along the base of 2,417' Willis Knob. This point is nearly 5 miles into the hike from Russell Bridge - the approximate halfway point between junctions.

Over the following mile, the path gradually descends to a point along the east bank of Warwoman Creek - a major Chattooga tributary. The trail crosses Warwoman via another ford - this one usually about knee-deep. Shortly beyond, primitive Earl's Ford Road is crossed before continuing westward. The trail closely parallels the creek for about 0.25 mile, then turns southwest toward its namesake river once again.

The trail intersects the river again about 0.5 mile below Warwoman Creek, closely following the riverbank for about 0.5 mile. The path then angles away from the river in the vicinity of the "Rock Garden" near the northern end of Section 3. A fairly short but rugged hike along the riverbank here will reveal dozens of huge granite boulders and slabs in the middle of the river, some leaning out over the current in near-identical form. This is truly one of the Chattooga's most scenic areas.

A half-mile beyond, the trail crosses Dick's Creek, another beautiful tributary. Be sure to check out the easy, short spur trail which runs down to one of the best views on the entire river - Dick's Creek Falls (see page 28). Everything comes together here and you would surely regret it if you missed this scene.

Below Dick's Creek, the path continues for 0.5 mile through a scenic, open hardwood forest before climbing slightly to a trail

junction. (Here the Bartram Trail turns and heads west toward Clayton and Warwoman Dell. The Chattooga River Trail continues south for an additional 10 miles before terminating - for now - at the Hwy 76 bridge about 8 miles southeast of Clayton). Several hundred yards west of the junction, the Bartram Trail crosses Sandy Ford Road. The Chattooga River Trail crosses Sandy Ford Road about 0.25 up from the river, just a short walk from Sandy Ford.
Directions to the various trailheads can be found on pages 26 and 27.

US 76 to Sandy Ford

Overview: Excellent day hike with several miles of riverside scenery. Numerous good camping sites. Described from south to north.
Trail Length: 10 miles
Difficulty: Moderate

The southernmost section of the Chattooga River Trail gently winds 10 miles from the heavily traversed US 76 bridge southeast of Clayton up to Sandy Ford. This portion of the path travels closely alongside its namesake for about 2 of the total 10 miles, but is always close to the river - usually no more than a quarter mile or so.

The trail currently originates (plans are being discussed for an extension south to Tallulah Falls State Park) in the small paved parking area along the northwest corner of the bridge behind several vehicle-blocking boulders. Throughout its length, the trail is blazed with white diamonds.

The initial half-mile ascends gradually up to a small bridge crossing spunky Pole Creek. Across, the path winds along the steeply sloped and heavily wooded mountainside, far above the crashing river well below.

Several miles into the hike the trail begins a long, gradual descent which brings the path within close proximity to the river while turning east. This descent terminates after a crossing of two small creeks. Shortly beyond, the trail turns sharply north - away from the river, and initiates a pulse-quickening climb of

The Rabun County Outdoors Companion

several hundred feet. This climb negotiates a low ridgeline just west of the Fall Creek junction along Section 3. This stretch of trail shortcuts a long wide riverbend. Someone evidently had the idea of trading scenery for time and distance. As the path descends from the ridge it intersects the river at mile 5.5.

Finally - river lovers rejoice! Enjoy the next 2 miles as it closely follows the river, allowing hikers easy access to dozens of sandy beaches and small, playful shoals. Although there are no major rapids, the scenery is outstanding and several good camping spots can be found close to the trail.

Beginning at mile 7.0, the trail again leaves the riverbank, undulating through the hilly terrain for the next several miles. Here the path again shortcuts a major bend in the river, only to return to the riverbank across from Second Ledge, one of Section 3's most exciting drops. Explore along the bank and find a good vantage point to watch boaters as they fall over this 6 foot sheer ledge.

Beyond Second Ledge, the path turns north and heads away from the river yet again. Several hundred yards beyond, the trail negotiates picturesque Rock Creek. Just beyond, the pathway crosses Sandy Ford Road. To the right and downhill, a several hundred yard walk will deposit you onto the beautiful open beach at Sandy Ford. Across the road, another 0.3 mile northwest is the junction with the Bartram Trail. To the north, the combined trails lead to Russell Bridge, some 10 miles distant. To the west, the Bartram Trail climbs over seemingly endless ridges toward Warwoman Dell just east of Clayton.

Directions to these trailheads can be found on pages 27 and 31.

The Lower Chattooga

General location: Generally located about 10 - 12 miles southeast of Clayton.

Overview: This portion of the river on the Georgia side is a bit difficult to access, but features a great deal of interesting scenery and some challenging backcountry hiking opportunities. The Raven Rock Trail features a magnificent cliff and river-wide ledge, while the Camp Creek area is tantalizingly close to the infamous Five Falls Section of the Chattooga.

Raven Rock Trail

Overview: Interesting short hike features massive Raven Rock Cliffs and Raven's Chute, a class IV rapid.
Trail Length: 0.8 mile
Difficulty: Moderate

Raven Rock cliffs is a worthy destination for anyone wishing to explore the middle portion of the Chattooga's Section 4 from the Georgia side. The initial 0.6 mile descends gently through a mixed hardwood forest conveniently along an old roadbed. This path is wide and generous, and helpful white diamond blazes guide the way.

At the 0.6 mile point, the path begins a steep descent into the heart of the rugged Chattooga gorge. Portions of the trail have been cut into the mountainside and reinforced with logs, creating manmade stairsteps. Other stretches loop along broad, gentle switchbacks. Occassional glimpses of the river far below will greatly whet your appetite to explore this scenic area.

At the base of the mountain, a large flat bottom relatively clear of underbrush invites campers to enjoy the peaceful setting beneath massive hemlocks and stately pines. Numerous old fire-rings attest to the past and present popularity of this area.

Only 25 yards away from this peaceful spot the restless Chattooga pounds through the rock-strewn gorge beneath towering Raven Cliffs, a near-200 foot escarpment of grey broken rock. A short boulder-hopping hike 100 yards upriver will provide you with a good look at the class IV plunge known as Raven's Chute. It's always exciting to watch whitewater daredevils race down the narrow chute along the far South Carolina bank.

Hikers can scramble up onto the ledge which forms the drop and gaze far upstream to glimpse Deliverance Rock, a huge river-blocking boulder. It is possible to pick your way upriver from here, but the heavy undergrowth and rough terrain make it very difficult.

From the Tallulah Falls bridge, head north on Hwy 441 for 3 miles. Turn right onto Camp Creek Road and proceed 2 miles to FS 511 on the left. Follow FS 511 for 3 miles to FS 511-B on the left. Follow FS 511-B for 0.8 mile to its deadend. The trail picks up here on the east end of the clearing. Warning: FS 511-B may be nearly impassable after heavy rains.

Camp Creek Trail

Overview: Short hike featuring good river access, several good camping spots and scenic Camp Creek.
Trail Length: 0.5 mile
Difficulty: Moderate

The Camp Creek Trail is really more of an access point than a real trail, yet this portion of the Chattooga is very much worth exploring. The path begins at the base of a broad parking area and descends 0.25 mile to the river in an area just above the Chattooga's wildest whitewater. A narrow strip of forest parallels this portion of the Chattooga, aptly nicknamed by boaters as the "Calm-Before-the-Storm".

Along the riverbank are several small sandy beaches that prove popular with boaters, hikers and fishermen. Beautiful Camp Creek merges with the Chattooga shortly downstream.

Several interesting scenes from the film "Deliverance" were filmed along this part of Camp Creek, and the beautiful moss-covered rocks and fern splashed banks create a scene which is popular with anyone lucky enough to visit here.

Several hundred yards below Camp Creek is the legendary "Five Falls" section of the Chattooga. Here, the river plunges almost 75 feet in a series of five back-to-back rapids. No real trail runs to the area, though the previous edition of this book described the bushwhacking trip. It is possible to get there, but the "hike" involves a good deal of scrambling through thick underbrush as well as climbing along steep slopes, root-grabbing and rock-hopping. It can be a bruising trip, though the scenery is surely spectacular. It is also a potentially dangerous trip.

The better route into Five Falls is from the South Carolina side. As of this printing, a newly revised Opossum Creek Trail was nearing completion which will access this area much more easily and safely. The old Opossum Creek Trail was largely destroyed by the Palm Sunday 1994 tornado which flattened a large portion of the lower river corridor.

Directions: Follow the directions to Raven Cliffs. Instead of turning left onto FS 511-B, continue on FS-511 and follow until it deadends, about 4 miles from Camp Creek Road.

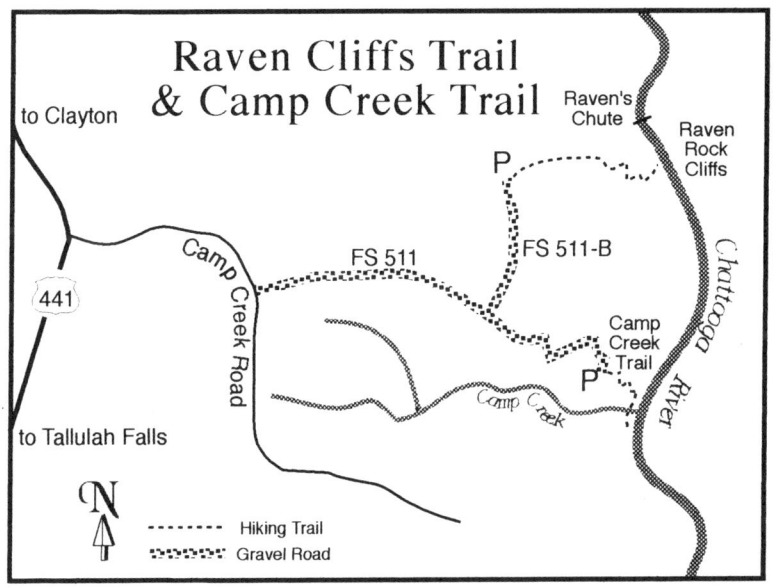

Chattooga River - Whitewater Boating Information

Section II

Overview: Excellent stretch for beginning whitewater boaters. Features several class 2 rapids, one class 3
Length: 7 miles
Difficulty: Moderately Easy
Note: All floaters must register and comply with Forest Service floating regulations before embarking on any Chattooga trip.

Section II is a relatively calm and scenic 7 mile paddle running from Russell Bridge down to Earl's Ford. Mild whitewater is the rule here, with one class 3 drop - Big Shoals - in the middle of the run. This section combines easy access, forgiving rapids and outstanding scenery to create an ideal beginners section, and an attractive run for experienced boaters as well. Section II is a good choice for almost any type of watercraft - canoes, kayaks, rafts or innertubes.

Section III

Overview: Magnificent scenery and moderate level whitewater. Extremely popular, though not for beginners!
Length: 12.5 miles
Difficulty: Moderate
Note: All floaters must register and comply with Forest Service floating regulations before embarking on any Chattooga trip.

Section III is undoubtedly one of the most popular whitewater runs in the Southeast, and perhaps the nation. The river flows unimpeded for almost 13 stunningly beautiful miles, from Earl's

Ford to the Hwy 76 bridge. For whitewater buffs, Section III means outstanding mountain scenery combined with challenging whitewater that reaches a class 5 crescendo at Bull Sluice. Section 3 is much more difficult than Section II. The current is much stronger, the rapids more numerous and technical, and access more difficult. Paddling skills must be of an intermediate to advanced level to be on the safe side. Guided trips and rentals are offered locally. Check in the information section of this book for names and numbers of local outfitters.

Section IV

Overview: Difficult and dangerous, this is one of the premier whitewater runs in the country. Great scenery, awesome whitewater - what more could you ask for?
Length: 7 miles
Difficulty: Difficult
Note: All floaters must register and comply with Forest Service floating regulations before embarking on any Chattooga trip.

Section IV is about as good as it gets if whitewater is your passion. Even though the Chattooga is not a large river, its intense drop-and-pool nature creates some legendary whitewater action. This seven mile stretch plunges wildly, averaging 45 feet per mile from the US 76 bridge down to Lake Tugaloo. Narrow rock-strewn gorges, sheer cliffs and wild waterfalls are only a taste of what this extremely beautiful section offers.

Boaters come here from all over the country to test this "experts only" whitewater. The river requires excellent whitewater skills, and can be quite exhausting due to the scouting involved.

Like Section III, several local outfitters offer guided trips on this spectacular stretch of river. Check on page 80 of this guide for names and numbers.

Section 3
Rabun County's
National Forest Service Hiking Trails & Attractions

Southwest Rabun

Fall Branch Trail - Minnehaha Falls

Overview: Easy, short hike to one of Rabun County's most beautiful cascades.
Trail Length: 0.3 mile one way
Difficulty: Easy
Hazards: Slippery rocks around the base. Stay off the falls!

Spectacular Minnehaha Falls, long a personal favorite and one of Rabun County's most well known and accessible cascades, lies at the end of an easy 0.3 mile trail just off popular Lake Rabun's wooded southern shoreline. The word "Minnehaha" is Cherokee for "laughing waters" and is certainly Rabun's most appropriately named cascade.

The path leading back to Minnehaha begins on the south side of Bear Gap Road. The Forest Service has recently replaced the old trail marker with a new sign just about impossible to miss. Whereas Minnehaha's trailhead used to be a challenge to find, visitors should no longer have a problem. The initial hundred yards climbs gradually through a thick hillside grove of laurel and rhododendron which reach a crescendo of color and fragrance in late spring and early summer. The remainder of the distance to the falls is mostly level, though the path does scramble up a low bank near the cascade. Several hundred feet below the trail lively Fall Branch serenades your stroll.

The trail ends on a flat grey slab of granite below the falls. This rock provides an excellent (and safe) observation point from which to enjoy this magnificent 60 foot cascade. Below the main drop another series of steep slides rush among the choking streamside rhododendron. The upper cascades are particularly photogenic during the above mentioned blooming season. Minnehaha Falls is a special place - perfect for anything from a short stroll to a lingering picnic - be sure not to miss it!

The Rabun County Outdoors Companion

Directions: Proceed north from Tallulah Falls to the first bridge crossing the Tallulah River. Turn left here onto old Hwy 441 (there should be a sign indicating mileage to Rabun Beach Recreation Area). Proceed 2.5 miles to the next intersection, then turn left again and follow winding Lake Rabun Road 5.5 miles to the road on your left which crosses the lake/river several hundred yards below the Seed Lake dam. Cross this bridge, then veer left onto Bear Gap Road. Proceed 1.6 miles to the gravel pull-off on the left. The trailhead is marked currently by a prominent Forest Service sign. See road map page 50.

Beautiful Minnehaha Falls along the short Fall Branch Trail

Joe Branch Trail - Angel Falls

Overview: Short hike leading to two small cascades.
Trail Length: 1.2 miles one way
Difficulty: Easy to Moderate. Trail gains approximately 700 feet.
Hazards: Several portions of the trail have steep drop-offs. Slippery rocks around the falls.
Note: Falls may virtually disappear during extended dry spells.

This relatively easy and thoroughly enjoyable 1 mile trail follows small but scenicly entertaining Joe Branch northward from Rabun Beach Recreation Area camping area #2, offering hikers close up views of two small but picturesque waterfalls. This heavily shaded trail climbs easily through dense groves of streamside rhododendron past enormous oaks, poplars and hemlocks. Wildflowers are prevalent in season, but the path is unusually inviting from late fall through early spring when the barren hardwoods offer probing views of the narrow gorge.

The initial 0.9 mile along this trail features several stream crossings before reaching pretty Panther Falls. This stairstepping 50 foot drop tumbles intricately over a series of stratified ledges. Although the uppermost cascades are hidden, the near symmetrical lower ledges create a picturesque setting.

Above Panther Falls the trail climbs steeply, passing Panther's upper cascades as it climbs further up the narrow valley. Take care here, as steep slopes crowd the narrow, slippery path. Angel Falls is another 600 yards beyond, though the distance seems longer due to the increased steepness of the trail above Panther Falls. Angel Falls is located along a loop at the trail's end.

Angel Falls offers quite a different visual experience, tumbling about 60 feet over a wide, steep rock face. Tiny Joe Branch is diluted across the rocky ledge, creating an intricate series of sparkling drops. A small observation platform provides the perfect vantage point.

The hike back downstream will undoubtedly seem much shorter. Take your time and savor the forest, the creek and all that this pleasant area has to offer.

The Rabun County Outdoors Companion

Directions: From Tallulah Falls, proceed north for 3 miles and turn left onto old Hwy 441 (there should be a Forest Service sign here marking the turn). Proceed 2.5 miles to the next intersection. Turn left here onto Lake Rabun Road and follow the winding road 4.5 miles to the Rabun Beach Recreation Area's camping area #2. Turn right into the campground and follow the loop to the northern end and the signs marking the trailhead.

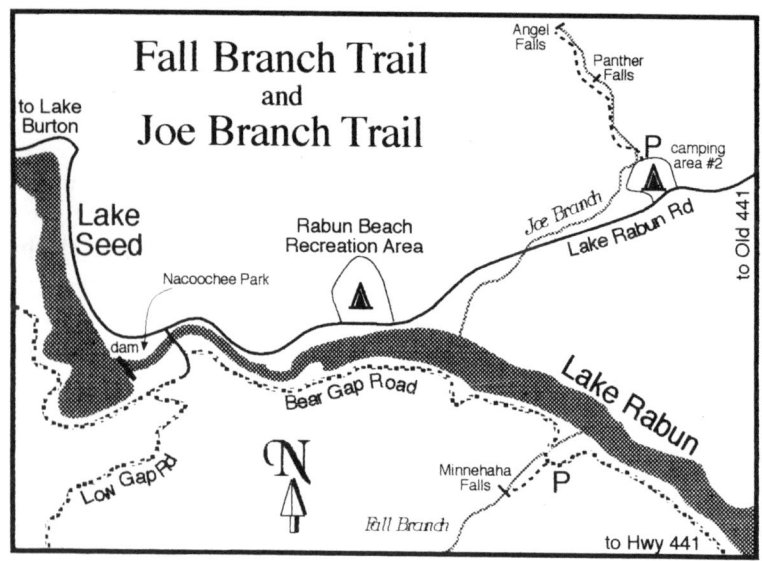

Central Rabun

Becky Branch Falls Loop Trail

Overview: Short hike to pleasant cascade.
Trail Length: 0.25 mile loop trail
Difficulty: Moderate
Hazards: Several steep drops along trail.

Becky Branch Falls, located only 5 minutes from Clayton in historic Warwoman Dell Recreation Area, is one of the most accessible cascades in Rabun County. Even the most novice hiker will enjoy the short (but steep) loop trail which crosses just a few feet from the base of this charming cascade.

The easier route is to follow the trail from Warwoman Dell up to Warwoman Road, cross the road, then take the path on the right side of the creek. This option allows hikers to take advantage of a few switchbacks cut into the mountain, greatly reducing the huffing and puffing required in the 150' foot climb to the falls. Be aware that the Bartram Trail branches to the right off this leg of the loop. The waterfall loop always stays within sight of Becky Branch.

A wooden footbridge crosses Becky Branch just beneath the splashing falls. From here, it's all downhill through a beautiful hardwood forest featuring plenty of fragrant rhododendron along the stream bed. The pathway emerges from the forest along Warwoman Road just across the creek from the original portion of the trail leading up to the falls.

Directions: From Hwy 441 in Clayton, take Warwoman Road east for 2.4 miles to Warwoman Dell Recreation Area. Park here and follow the Bartram Trail north to the waterfall loop.

Warwoman Dell Nature Trail

Overview: Self-guided interpretive nature trail
Trail Length: 0.4 mile loop trail
Difficulty: Easy

Normally unknown to visitors to Warwoman Dell is the enjoyable nature trail which loops through the western end of the recreation area. This self-guided pathway features several dozen stations describing various natural features. The trail crosses tiny Warwoman Creek several times along the interesting walkway. While not dramatic, the trail is nonetheless both interesting and educational.

Directions: Warwoman Dell is located 2.4 miles east of Clayton on Warwoman Road.

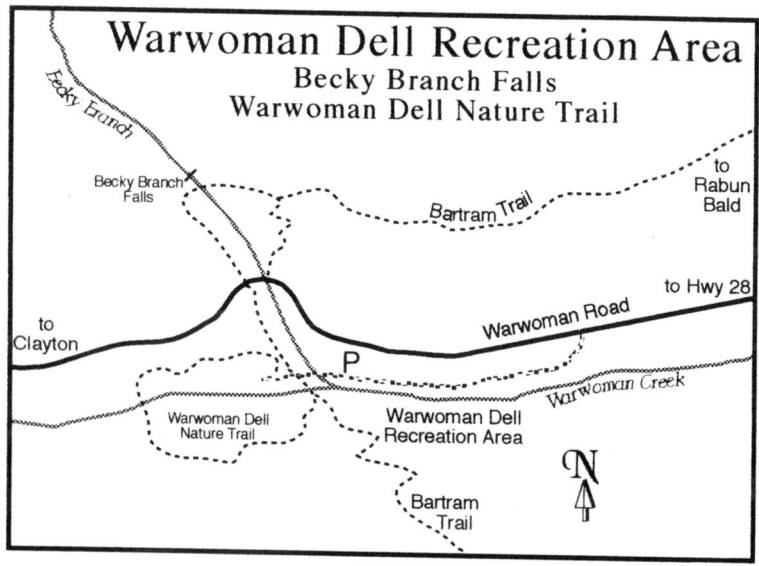

Northwest Rabun

Patterson Creek Falls

Overview: Very short scramble down to series of small falls.
Trail Length: 100 yards or less
Difficulty: Moderate
Hazards: No maintained trail, slippery rocks.

    Patterson Creek Falls, also known as Laurel Falls, is yet another Rabun County waterfall relatively easy to visit. These falls tumble along noisy Patterson Creek deep within a secluded grove of thick rhododendron and laurel. This waterfall is actually an extended series of small falls and cascades which drop perhaps 100 feet, with several respectable individual cascades. A worn network of paths run alongside the creek, making access to most of the drops a moderately easy scramble.

    Directions: From Hwy 441 in downtown Dillard, turn west onto Betty's Creek Road and proceed 3.5 miles to Patterson Gap Road on the left. Drive 0.5 mile and park on the shoulder. Find one of the overgrown paths that descend toward the sound of falling water.

Grassy Ridge Trail

Overview: Appalachian spur trail featuring excellent vistas and a wide variety of plant life.
Trail Length: 2.5 miles one way to Carter's Gap
Difficulty: Moderate

    The Grassy Ridge Trail, best known to Rabun County hunters, runs along the crest of scenic Grassy Ridge for 2.5 miles from Patterson Gap to the Appalachian Trail at North Carolina's Car-

The Rabun County Outdoors Companion

ter Gap. This high, dry ridge also follows the Tennessee Valley Divide northward into the Nantahalas.

The massive Southern Nantahala Wilderness Area stretches westward from this trail, which also borders the Coleman River Wildlife Management Area. Coleman WMA signs announce your arrival at Patterson Gap, and several small dirt pull-offs provide parking. During prime hunting season, which is not the best time to hike, pickup trucks can be parked all across the gap. The trail begins in the gap following an old roadbed northward up the ridge.

Approximately 0.3 mile from the trailhead, a fork to the right winds over to the beautiful, north facing Till Ridge Cove. *The Georgia Conservancy's Guide to the North Georgia Mountains* describes this cove as one of the richest botanical areas in the state, with tremendous seasonal displays of wildflowers.

The left fork of the main trail continues atop the ridge, attaining lofty elevations above 4,400 feet before turning northwest beyond Nichol's Gap at mile 1.5. The trail continues an additional mile beyond the gap, undulating along the slopes of massive Ridgepole Mountain before crossing into North Carolina and reaching the Appalachian Trail at Carter Gap.

Directions: From Hwy 441 in downtown Dillard, follow Betty's Creek Road west for 3.5 miles to Patterson Gap Road (FS 32) on the left. Proceed along the winding, bumpy gravel road for 3.6 miles to Patterson Gap.

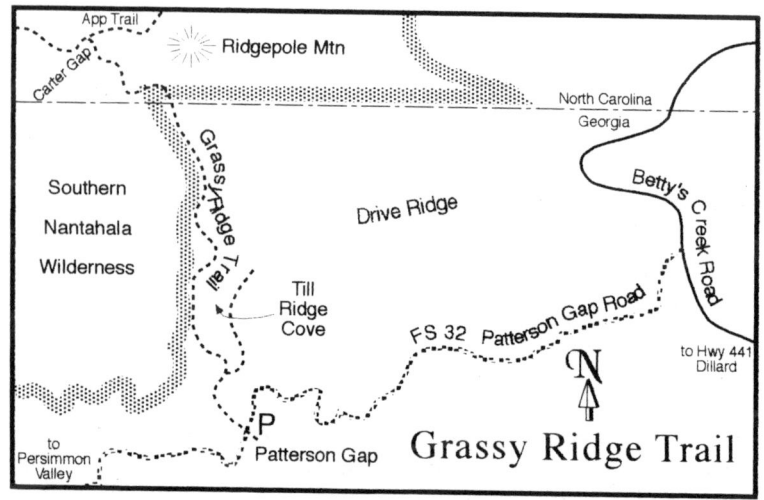

The Rabun County Outdoors Companion

Tate City

General location: Tate City is about 12 miles northwest of Clayton, though actual driving mileage is closer to 20 miles. **Though Tate City is not in Rabun County**, its extremely close proximity rates mentioning it here (besides the fact that it's darn near impossible to get there except through Rabun County).

Overview: Simply put, this is an area of superlatives. Here, Forest Service Road 70 closely follows the rugged Tallulah River through its upper watershed and into the Southern Nantahala Wilderness. Several forest service camping areas are featured, as well as numerous excellent hiking trails. This area is extremely popular with trout fishermen. See map page 60.

For many years Tate City was a busy mining and logging town situated in a lonely valley far removed from the rest of civilization. Nowadays, only a few dozen families make their homes in this beautifully peaceful setting, interupted only by the occasional tourist sightseeing in the valley. Rabun County visitors know this place quite well, and many have been enjoying Tate City for years.

One of the main attractions of this fascinating area is the drive itself. Three miles of FS 70 (Tallulah River Road) head straight up rugged Rock Gorge. This section of road was blasted from the mountainside and originally held a timber hauling railroad bed. Through this fantastically rugged section the Tallulah roars and rumbles over countless falls between mammoth grey boulders. Several pull-outs provide parking for you to stop and enjoy the outstanding scenery.

Several miles above the Rock Gorge, the road enters the narrow valley that is Tate City. Several small farms and numerous homes dot the valley and surrounding mountains. One can't help but marvel at the rugged individualism that the first settlers here must have exhibited, as you may feel an extreme sense of isolation here even today.

The Rabun County Outdoors Companion

Above Tate City, the valley narrows dramatically again as it enters into North Carolina. The road winds an additional two miles up the gorge before ending at a series of trailheads. All in all, FS 70 has taken you almost 9 miles since its starting point back on Persimmon Road.

From Clayton, proceed west on US 76 for 8 miles to Persimmon Road on the right. Proceed along Persimmon for 4 miles to Tallulah River Road (FS 70) on the left.

Coleman River Trail

Overview: Enjoyable short hike along scenic Coleman River.
Trail Length: 1.8 miles round trip
Difficulty: Easy to moderate.
Hazards: Several steep drop-offs, slippery rocks, roots on trail.

The Coleman River Trail may not make anybody's top ten list, but it is a worthy short trail if you enjoy the beauty of a sparkling mountain stream. To call Coleman a river is stretching it a bit, but this lively creek makes up in spirit what it may lack in actual size.

One of many small falls and pools along scenic Coleman River

The trail begins at the Coleman River bridge, and closely follows the river upstream past dozens of small shoals and lively ledges through a beautiful hardwood forest sprinkled with mature pines and hemlocks. Several moderate grades will get your heart pumping, but nothing major to worry about.

Much of the watershed is quite steep and narrow, but a few spots offer enough flat ground to allow for a nice picnic - Coleman River style. The trail dead-ends about 0.9 mile upstream of the bridge, though it is quite evident that many visitors explore upstream just a little further.

The trail begins at the Coleman River bridge - the first bridge encountered on FS 70 - about 1.7 miles from Persimmon Road. See map on page 60.

Denton Branch Falls

Overview: Short walk to scenic waterfall
Trail Length: 0.3 mile one way
Difficulty: Easy

One of the easiest sights to see in the Tate City area is a lively waterfall on lower Denton Branch. From one of the small pull-offs just before the ford on Denton Branch, cross the creek on foot and proceed beyond several vehicle blocking earthen mounds. Follow the old roadbed about 0.2 mile through mostly flat terrain until the road bends left. Here, follow a trail which branches off to the right, roughly following the creek. Proceed about 250 yards to the base of the falls (about 100 yards beyond the wilderness boundary markers).

A small island is formed by the splitting of the creek, providing a front row seat to this noisy, surprisingly powerful 25 foot drop. The rock face over which the waterfall spills extends to the left of the falls, and plenty of dripping water completes this wild scene.

Directions: The turn off to the falls (Denton Branch Road) is 6.6 miles up FS 70 (Tallulah River Road) from Persimmon Road. Turn right and head up the bumpy road for about .15 mile to the parking pull-off preceeding the creek crossing. See map on page 60.

Beech Creek Gorge

Overview: Highly scenic hike through a magnificent mountain gorge. Features several excellent waterfalls and plenty of outstanding scenery.
Trail Length: 2.25 miles one way to High Falls, other options.
Difficulty: Moderate to Strenuous

This excellent trail is a local favorite. Beech Creek Gorge ties into several other local trails as well as providing access to the Appalachian Trail. Numerous hiking possibilities make this very popular among serious hikers.

From FS 70, follow trail #378 (Beech Creek Trail) to the east up and over Scaly Ridge. The path then descends to beautiful Beech Creek near 0.5 mile. Several hundred feet across the creek the trail intersects an old logging road. Turn left here and follow the roadbed another 0.5 mile to where Bull Cove Creek flows across the road.

A primitive path runs upstream along the north bank of Bull Cove Creek up to Bull Cove Falls - a scenic 40 foot cascade. The waterfall is only 100 yards or so from the main trail - well worth the diversion. The cascade is a powerful fluming drop, exploding wildly into a narrow, rocky creekbed.

Beyond Bull Cove Creek, the main trail climbs slightly before fording Beech Creek and entering the spectacular Beech Creek Gorge. The pathway climbs steadily for the next mile through the narrow, heavily forested gorge. Bear Creek Falls is encountered about 0.4 mile above the ford, with Bear Creek cascading down a steep, broken rock face before running across the trail and dropping into Beech Creek below. The waterfall consists mainly of a series of waterslides, several of which are hidden high above the trail. This particular stretch of path features numerous cascades, all originating high above and off to the hiker's left. Only those with a keen eye will glimpse these lesser falls, which are particularly well hidden in the warm summer months.

Near mile 2.0, the old remains of an old corundum mine are found alongside the trail. This signals the beginning of a series of switchbacks which climb the southeastern flanks of Big Scaly Mountain. Proceed to the beginning of the second switchback to the left and a sign (usually there) directs you down to mighty High Falls. This side trail drops several hundred yards over to the base of the falls. Be cautious, as this side path is narrow and quite slippery in spots. Those who have endured the long, hard hike will be rewarded with a magnificent display of tumbling water that relatively few people get to see. High Falls churns out impressively over a steep cliff almost 200 feet high.

On your way back down, be sure to pay particular attention to the outstanding beauty of this wild area. Ominous sheer cliffs rise high above you, and the entire hike through the gorge is accompanied by the soft serenading of beautiful Beech Creek. Be sure to consult other hiking guides and topo maps - you'll be amazed at how many trip possiblilites there are involving the Beech Creek Trail. Though this trail isn't in Rabun County, it would be a shame not to include it for those visiting the Tate City area.

Directions: From Persimmon Road, follow FS 70 for 7.8 miles (0.4 miles past the NC line). Park in the clearing on the left side of the road. The trail marker and trailhead are on the east side of the road. See map on page 60.

The Tallulah River along the road to Tate City.

The Rabun County Outdoors Companion

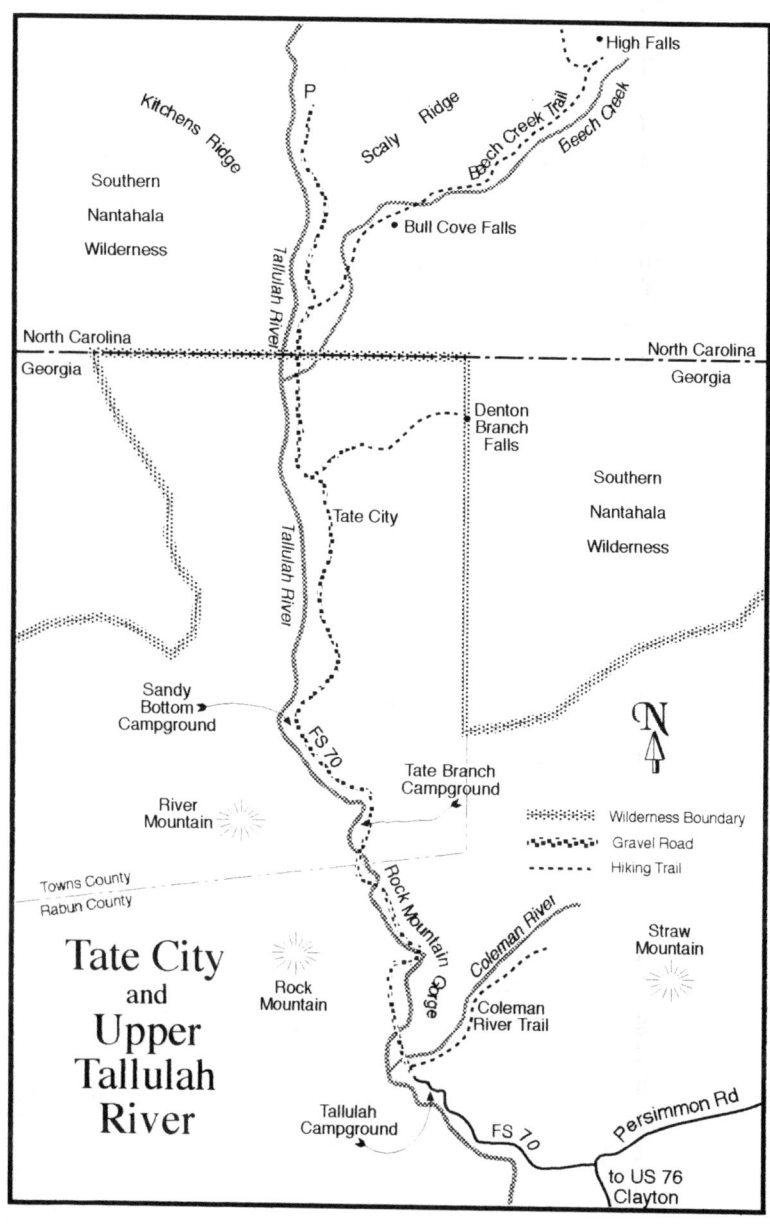

Appalachian Trail - Section 5

Trail Length: 16.6 mile section from Unicoi Gap to Dick's Creek Gap. Northernmost 8.4 miles straddles the Towns/Rabun County line.
Difficulty: Moderate to Strenuous

Quite unlike most of the trails in Rabun County, this portion of the famed Appalachian Trail is a non-stop roller coaster. Instead of closely following some scenic stream back to a secluded waterfall, this legendary pathway negotiates a seemingly endless series of peaks and gaps, much like the remainder of its 2,100 miles from Georgia's Springer Mountain to Maine's Mt. Katahdin. Elevations along this section range from 2,675' in Dick's Creek Gap to 4,430' atop Tray Mountain, making for an exhilarating hike.

This particular section, known as Georgia's Section 5, features 8.4 miles of trail along the Rabun/Towns County line. A few miles of Section 6 also run through Rabun County. For a more thorough description of either section, consult one of the seemingly dozens of Appalachian Trail guides.

Section 5 makes an ideal 2 day hike, with camping spots abundant and water somewhat plentiful (One of the better water sources is at mile 5.5, where a side trail runs down to a shelter and spring). Perhaps the greatest attraction along this segment are the dozens of superb overlooks atop the scenic peaks and ridgelines. The finest along Section 5 is undoubtedly the rocky summit of Tray Mountain at 4,430'. Tray is the second highest AT summit in Georgia, and offers a magnificent panorama of the surrounding wilderness.

The 5.8 mile section between Tray Mountain and Addis Gap cuts through the heart of the 10,400 acre Tray Mountain Wilderness. The 5.4 mile section from Addis Gap to Dick's Creek Gap parallels the dividing line for two vast game management areas. To the west is the massive 19,000 acre Swallow Creek Wildlife Management Area. To the east is the 12,600 acre Lake Burton Wildlife Management Area.

Directions: The Unicoi Gap trailhead is nine miles north of Helen on Highway 17/75. Dick's Creek Gap is 16 miles west of Clayton on Highway 76.

The Rabun County Outdoors Companion

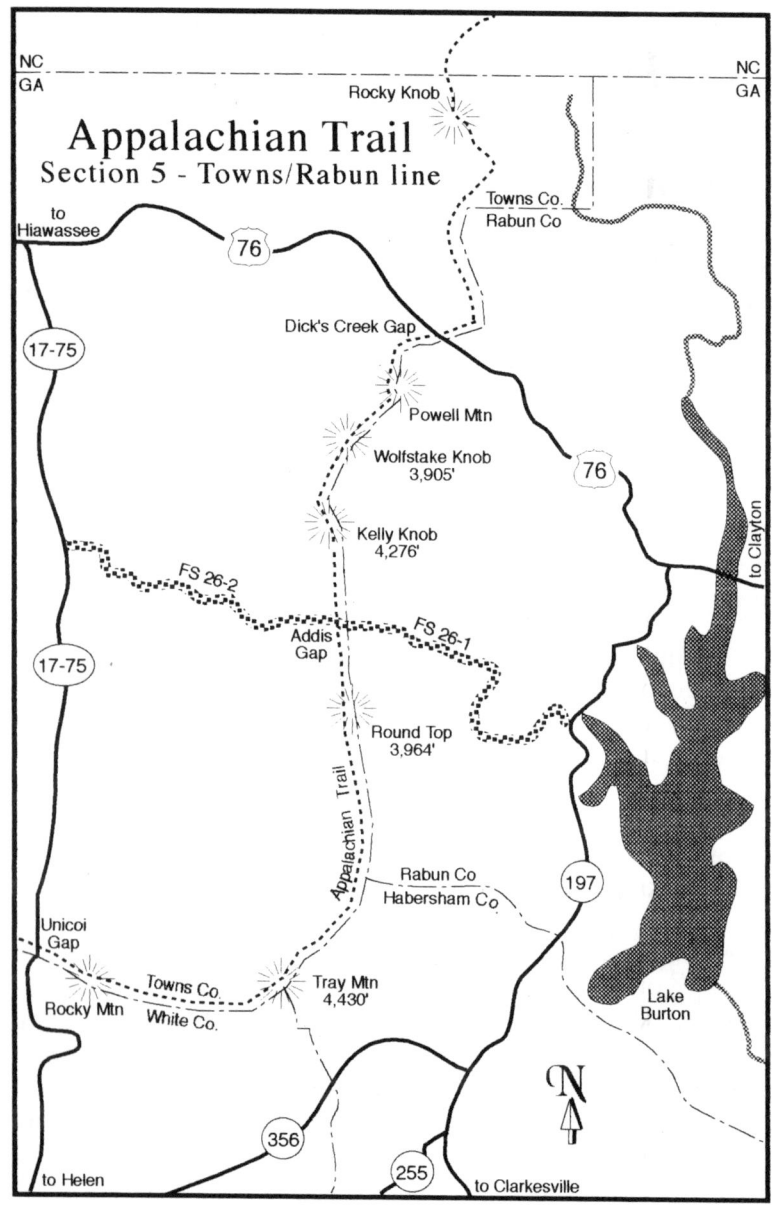

Northeast Rabun

Rabun Bald

Overview: Extremely popular hike leading to Georgia's second highest summit.
Trail Length: 3.0 mile round trip
Difficulty: Moderate - 1,000 foot elevation gain.

Beautiful Rabun Bald guards Georgia's northeast corner, and at 4,696' is the state's second highest mountain peak. Surpassed in height only by 4,784' Brasstown Bald, Rabun Bald offers a refreshingly different experience from the crowds atop some of the region's more well known summits. The combination of lack of facilities and the difficulty in finding the trailhead combine to make Rabun Bald one of the very best of Rabun's wild places.

The hike to Rabun Bald's summit offers a number of options (see end of this narrative). Two relatively short routes are available, and most visitors choose one of these. One is to begin at Bee Gum Gap and follow a spur trail along an old roadbed. This path soon merges with the popular Bartram Trail and ascends 1.5 miles to the summit. A quicker and easier route follows an old, bumpy gravel road through Bee Gum Gap up to a tiny parking area below the summit. The Bartram Trail comes alongside this parking area before rising for another 0.5 mile to the mountain's peak.

Take your choice, but be aware that the gravel road leading up to the parking area is extremely primitive and contains some pretty severe bumps, potholes and washouts. Think twice unless you have a rugged four-wheel drive vehicle. Both routes traverse the beautiful, shady hardwood forests along Rabun Bald's cool northern slopes.

Above this upper parking area the Bartram Trail snakes through a series of moderately steep switchbacks, gaining altitude rapidly through lush rhododendron thickets. The pathway straightens and flattens somewhat once it attains the ridgeline that makes up the summit, and soon emerges into the open bald

The Rabun County Outdoors Companion

atop the ancient peak. Here at the base of a newly renovated stone observation tower, the Bartram Trail reaches a junction with the Three Forks Trail merging from the east.

The old stone tower reaches about 20 feet into the air and well above the surrounding vegetation. A magificent 360° panorama offers visitors a breathtaking vista. Dozens of rugged forested peaks and serene valleys unfurl before you. Steep, rocky peaks in the Nantaha range to the north compete with rolling ridgelines to the east and south. Sky Valley is plainly visible below to the west. Truly this is a spot to linger and enjoy. Rabun Bald is a real sleeper among Georgia's peaks, and is definitely recommended if you want to get off the beaten path.

Additional hikes: Rabun Bald's summit can also be reached by the Three Forks Trail from the east and the Bartram Trail from both the north and south. The Three Forks Trail is a steep, challenging 6 mile round trip from Hale Ridge Road (FS 7). The Three Forks trail extends beyond Hale Ridge for another 6 miles before terminating along the banks of the scenic West Fork at rugged Three Forks. The various road crossings and trails in the area provide plenty of options depending on your skill level and stamina.

The Bartram Trail also crosses Hale Ridge Road north of Rabun Bald before winding up to Bee Gum Gap and proceeding up to the summit. The total trail distance from Hale Ridge Road to Warwoman Dell east of Clayton is 17.5 miles.

Directions: From Dillard, proceed north on Hwy 441 to Ga. Hwy 246. Turn right onto Hwy 246 and proceed 4.3 miles to the Sinclair station on the right and the sign directing you to Sky Valley. Turn right here and drive 2.8 miles to the gravel road on your right. There is a newly placed Forest Service sign here directing you to the trailhead. Proceed up this gravel road for 0.3 mile to Bee Gum Gap. Here you will see the road continue straight ahead to the upper parking area, and the spur trail beginning behind a vehicle-blocking mound of dirt to the left. If you leave your car in the gap, be sure to pull well off the road and lock your vehicle.

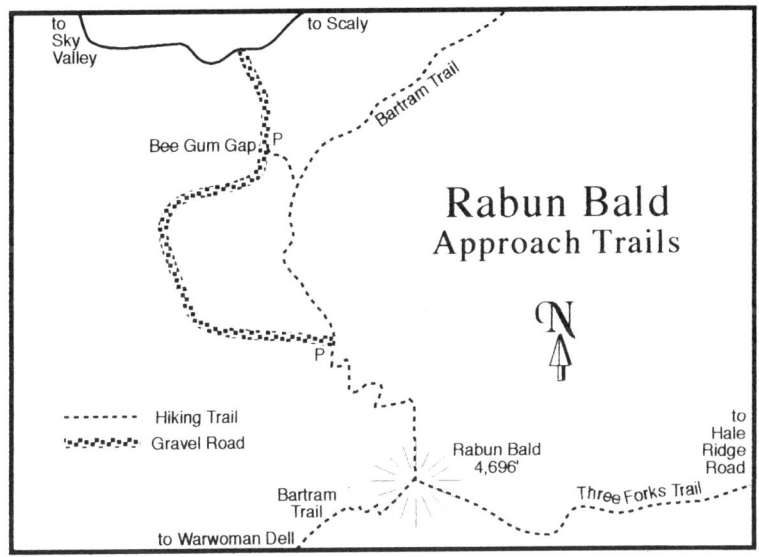

Holcomb Creek Trail

Overview: Very popular short hike featuring two beautiful cascades.
Trail Length: 0.6 mile to 1.6 miles, depending on route
Difficulty: Moderate

The magnificent Holcomb Creek Trail in northeast Rabun County features two scenic waterfalls along a highly enjoyable footpath completely engulfed within a pristine forest setting. From the main trailhead this pathway descends moderately through a series of switchbacks until beautiful Holcomb Creek Falls appears around a bend in the trail at mile 0.3. This spectacular cascade drops 120 feet with the uppermost cascades free-falling down a rugged rock face. Holcomb Creek then rushes between mammoth boulders before skirting beneath the wooden bridge along the trail. The bridge offers a convenient and safe location from which to photograph the falls.

The trail continues sidewalk flat beyond Holcomb for several hundred yards before climbing somewhat steeply for 0.2 mile to Ammons Creek Falls (notice the spur trail coming in from the left before you reach the falls). Ammons Creek Falls, also known as Emory Falls, spills over a steep rock face just yards from a stilted

The Rabun County Outdoors Companion

observation deck just yards from the falls. The total drop here is around 40 feet. Though not as spectacular as Holcomb Creek Falls, Ammons is well worth seeing.

Hikers may return to the trailhead the same route they came or the hike can be extended by following the spur trail below Ammons Falls 0.5 mile back up to Hale Ridge Road. This trail closely follows tumbling Holcomb Creek upstream and exits the forest 0.6 mile **up the road** from the original trailhead. You may choose to walk this trail as a complete loop or shorten the trip by parking a vehicle at each trailhead. The total loop distance is 1.6 miles. The shorter options offer a hike of about 1 mile.

Directions: From Hwy 441 in Clayton, proceed east on Warwoman Road for 7 miles to Hale Ridge Road (FS 7) on the left. Follow Hale Ridge Road for 6.8 miles to the intersection of Hale Ridge and Overflow Road (FS 86). Park here and look for the trailhead sign on the north side of the intersection.

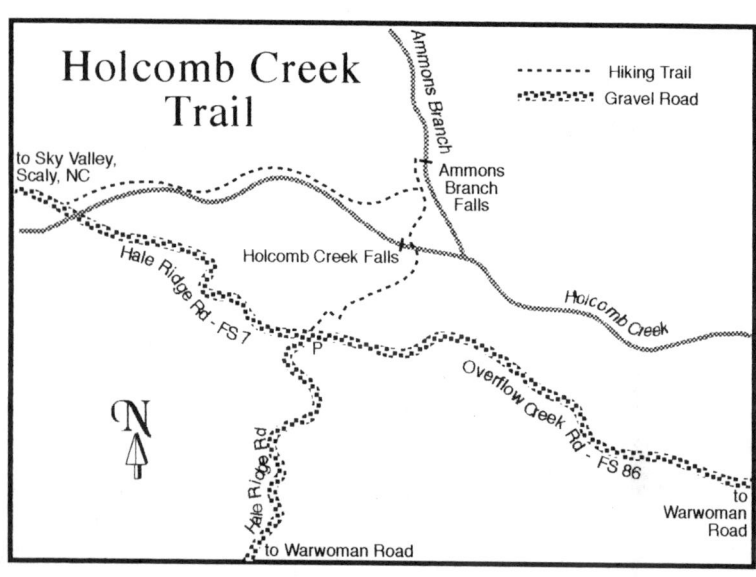

Three Forks Trail

Overview: Moderately strenuous hike to a highly scenic gorge along the West Fork.
Trail Length: 1.5 miles one way to Three Forks
Difficulty: Ranges from easy to difficult
Hazards: Slippery rocks, steep drop-offs

The Three Forks Trail in northeastern Rabun County is a true Jekyll and Hyde trail which can provide either an exciting or miserable hike, depending on your skill level and stamina. This highly scenic path captures most of the true wilderness character all hikers long for - isolation, pristine forest, abundant wildlife, gorgeous scenery. For this reason, Three Forks has become a relatively popular destination, though it takes a great deal of effort to reach.

The novice hiker may wish to tackle the one mile hike one-way to the small, powerful cascade on Holcomb Creek above Three Forks. From the parking area at John Teague Gap, this

Three Forks - Looking down toward the West Fork from the brink of a small falls on Holcomb Creek.

white-blazed trail meanders gently along a high, dry ridge featuring broad vistas to the north. Far below, the roaring of rushing Holcomb Creek serves to spark your interest. Approximately 0.9 mile from the trailhead, a gradual descent drops the path onto an old jeep road.

To reach the small falls on Holcomb Creek, turn left and follow the rutted road down toward the sound of rushing water. The trail ends on a large rock ledge at the brink of a fluming cascade. Of special interest are the many potholes created by powerful swirling currents. **Use extreme caution while exploring this area** - the rocks here are very slippery and any fall here could prove to be serious! Upstream of this point, numerous sparkling cascades and clear, crystalline pools adorn this stretch of creek, long appreciated by trout fishermen and explorers alike.

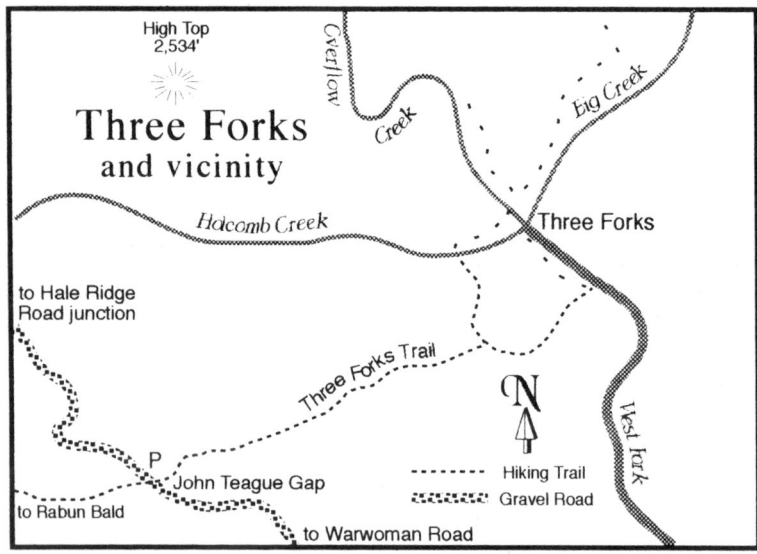

Several routes to Three Forks are possible, though none are particularly easy by any means. From the small falls on Holcomb Creek, hikers have two choices. The first option involves crossing the creek (safely above the falls) and looking for the faint signs of a path or paths that roughly follow the creek downstream. Several overgrown paths emerge along Overflow Creek, just above Three Forks. Some choose to pick their way downstream along the southern side of Holcomb Creek, but **use extreme caution due to numerous steep drop-offs**. Either way is a bit less than a quarter mile down to Three Forks, and none is particularly easy or completely safe.

The Rabun County Outdoors Companion

An additional route that is perhaps the easiest involves going back to the point where the trail and old jeep road meet at mile 0.9. From here, turn right and follow the trail uphill to the crest of the ridge. Scout around carefully and locate the primitive path that descends, seemingly straight down, to the West Fork below (careful - there are several dangerous cliffs in the area). Once alongside the river, you can pick your way up the riverbank to Three Forks, several hundred yards distant.

Despite the challenges, Three Forks is a very worthy destination. Here the West Fork of the mighty Chattooga is formed by the near right-angle confluence of Big Creek, Overflow Creek and Holcomb Creek. Holcomb Creek and Big Creek enter the junction over small, sparkling waterfalls. Overflow features its own majestic drop perhaps 0.4 mile upstream from Three Forks. Several excellent waterfalls can also be found along Big Creek. Locate and follow one of the primitive paths upstream from Three Forks to view these falls.

Mammoth boulders and sheer bluffs produce an imposing wilderness setting at Three Forks. Movement along the banks is somewhat slow and can be frustrating at times, but for any outdoorsman this is a great destination. For those hikers wishing a much longer and strenuous challenge, consider hiking the complete Three Forks Trail, which runs from the West Fork to the summit of Rabun Bald 9.5 miles distant.

Directions: From Hwy 441 in Clayton, take Warwoman Road east for 13.5 miles. Turn left onto Overflow Road (FS 86) just beyond the West Fork bridge and proceed 4 miles to John Teague Gap. There is a small parking area and normally a sign denoting the trailhead.

The Bartram Trail

Overview: Offers hikes ranging from short walks to multi-day trips featuring outstanding scenery.
Trail Length: 37 miles total in Rabun - see map page 73
Hale Ridge Road to Warwoman Dell - 17.5 miles
Warwoman Dell to Dick's Creek Road - 9.4 miles
Dick's Creek Road to Highway 28 - 9.8 miles
Difficulty: Ranges from easy to difficult

Rabun County's longest trail roughly retraces 18th century explorer and naturalist William Bartram's journey through the region in 1776. Bartram's extensive descriptions have enabled modern day explorers to recreate an extensive trail designed to follow the original journey undertaken over 200 years ago. Thirty seven miles of this delightful trail wind through Rabun County's northeast corner, offering hikers a tremendous wilderness experience. The path extends from Rabun northward into North Carolina and east into South Carolina.

Rabun County's portion of this well known trail enters the state from North Carolina just south of Osage Mountain. The trail climbs east of Sky Valley, skirting Bee Gum Gap before attaining the summit of mighty Rabun Bald (Georgia's second highest peak at 4,696'). Then begins a gradual descent over a prolonged series of peaks and gaps down to Warwoman Road nearly 13 miles distant.

Turning east, the trail gently negotiates a series of ridges and valleys before reaching Sandy Ford Road and the Chattooga River Trail junction over 9 miles away. The last leg of Rabun's Bartram section then heads northeast for almost 10 miles, roughly paralleling the Chattooga River up to a crossing at the Highway 28 bridge.

Hale Ridge Road to Warwoman Dell

Trail Length: 17.5 miles
Difficulty: Moderate to Strenuous

This grueling 17.5 miles is definitely the most difficult and strenuous of Rabun's portion of the Bartram. Here the trail is eerily similar to Rabun's nearby portion of the Appalachian Trail

The Rabun County Outdoors Companion

- namely a seemingly endless series of ascents and descents as the path climbs over peaks and descends into the accompanying gaps. This portion of the trail is a real joy to walk - and it's also a real calorie burner.

Elevation readings along the trail reflect the type of hike you can expect - 3,280' at Hale Ridge Road, 3,640' - Bee Gum Gap, 4,696' - Rabun Bald summit, 3,740' - Salt Rock Gap, 4,100' - Flat Top, 3,260' - Rock Mountain Gap, 3,680' - Rock Mountain, 1,920' - Warwoman Road.

The generally wide trail is well blazed and should be easy for hikers to follow. The path does utilize several short segments along dirt roads, and hikers must pay close attention to blazes and signs along these roads to keep from losing the trail.

Numerous scenic features stand out along this rugged portion of trail. Most notable is the panorama atop Rabun Bald from the newly renovated tower. Several other good vantage points can be found along the trail - especially the overlooks at Wilson Knob and Double Knob. Two small cascading falls are also found in the final two miles - a rushing 50 foot drop on Martin Creek at mile 15.6 and the beautiful cascade on Becky Branch mentioned separately in this guide. This portion of trail terminates at Warwoman Dell Recreation Area just east of Clayton. Consult USGS quadrangle maps for details.

This scene, taken from near Sky Valley, is typical of the views from the Bartram Trail near Rabun Bald..

The Rabun County Outdoors Companion

Warwoman Dell to Sandy Ford Road

Trail Length: 9.4 miles
Difficulty: Moderate

The middle segment of Rabun's Bartram Trail meanders some 9.4 miles east from Warwoman Dell over gently rolling ridges to a junction with the Chattooga River Trail west of Sandy Ford. This part of the trail offers a stark contrast from the roller-coaster peak-to-gap experience below Rabun Bald. Beautiful expanses of open forest are the primary attraction, with several good vistas available along the trail.

The pathway crosses several Forest Service roads in its journey east. Heading east from the dell, crossings occur at mile 1.5, 1.9, 5.9 (Pool Creek Road) and 7.2. Keep these access points in mind in case of emergency.

The gentle terrain along this portion of the trail is very appealing to overnighters who may choose from dozens of attractive camping spots. Old fire rings offer mute testimony to the scores of visitors who have enjoyed this particular portion of the trail.

Sandy Ford Road to Highway 28

Trail Length: 9.8 miles
Difficulty: Easy to Moderate

This moderately easy 9.8 mile section winds along the Chattooga River's west bank, generally within the quarter-mile wide Wild and Scenic River corridor. This portion of the trail is also a segment of the Chattooga River Trail. For a general description of this section, refer to page 37.

The Rabun County Outdoors Companion

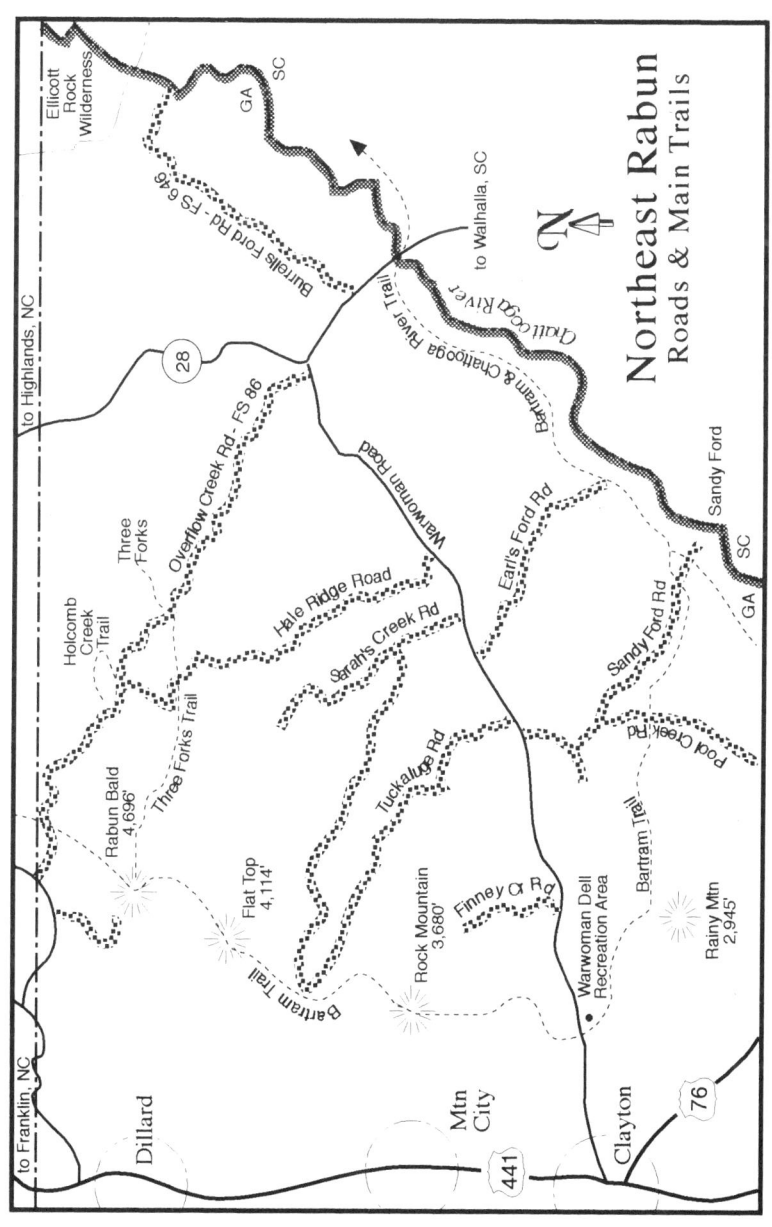

The Rabun County Outdoors Companion

Section 4
Rabun County
*Places to Go,
Sights to See,
Things to Do*

Estatoah Falls

Estatoah Falls is a large, open cascade prominently visible from Highway 246 just below Sky Valley. This magnificent drop of several hundred feet is privately owned, and though you can't walk to the base, the falls can nonetheless be enjoyed from your vehicle. While during dry conditions the falls may become almost non-existent, after a heavy rain the cascade booms from the sheer rockface.

Directions: From Dillard, take Highway 246 toward Sky Valley. After about one mile, look ahead, just off to the right side of the road. You should quickly notice the exposed rock cliff and falls on the lower slopes of the mountain before you.

Mud Creek Falls

Another prominent waterfall that can be enjoyed by everyone is the powerful cascade which explodes just downstream of the Sky Valley golf course. This beautiful waterfall - tragically named Mud Creek Falls - is a real sleeper among Rabun's cascades. The waterfall roars over a jagged 60 foot ledge, featuring a wild "roostertail" of exploding water. The upper 40 feet plunges almost straight down, while the lower 10 feet or so is over a stairstepping shoal. A perfectly placed picnic table accents the experience at the base.

Directions: Upon entering the Sky Valley resort, bear left and proceed 0.55 mile to Tahoe Road on the right. Drive 0.5 mile until the pavement ends, then continue an additional 0.25 mile along the gravel road down to the base of the falls.

The Lakes of the Tallulah River

Among the most beautiful of Rabun County's natural assets are its string of incomparable mountain lakes. Five manmade lakes along the Tallulah River create a string of jewels that stretch across the county. These lakes, created by Georgia Power with hydroelectric power in mind in the 1910's and 1920's, not only offer scenic homesites for some, but tremendous recreational opportunities both for Rabun residents and visitors.

The lakes - Burton, Seed, Rabun, Tallulah and Tugalo are each delightfully diverse and offer very different recreational experiences. Powerboating, sailing, skiing, swimming, fishing and canoeing are just a few of the leisure time activities you may enjoy on Rabun's lakes.

Lake Burton
Surface Area: 2,275 acres
Shoreline: 62 miles
Elevation: 1,867 feet
Dam: 128 feet high, 1,110 feet long, completed - 1919

Impounded in 1919, Lake Burton has long been popular with boaters and fishermen. This long, narrow lake has numerous fingers and coves, and can offer visitors a wide range of boating experiences. The lake is named for the old settlement and town of Burton which was submerged upon the lake's completion. The shoreline is heavily developed with private homes - if you're looking for a wilderness setting, better keep looking.

Nacoochee Lake
Surface Area: 240 acres
Shoreline: 13 miles
Elevation: 1,753 feet
Dam: 75 feet high, 490 feet long, completed - 1926

Nacoochee Lake's shoreline closely follows the original Tallulah River's course through the valley, and is predominately quite narrow. Nacoochee, most often referred to as Seed Lake, is 4.5 miles long and, like all the other lakes in this string, is quite popular with fishermen. Nacoochee is also a great lake for canoeing, since open areas of lake exposed to wind are minimal.

Lake Rabun
Surface Area: 834 acres
Shoreline: 25 miles
Elevation: 1,690 feet
Dam: 108 feet high, 660 feet long, completed- 1925

There are many who now feel that Lake Rabun is *the* most beautiful of Georgia's mountain lakes. Generations have also felt this way, as residents and visitors have been enjoying this lake since the late 1920's. Lake Rabun offers excellent vistas of the surrounding mountains and is a good choice for fishing, boating or canoeing. The shoreline is developed with private homes, but still retains the mountain setting which has made it so popular.

Tallulah Lake
Surface Area: 63 acres
Shoreline: 3.6 miles
Elevation: 1,500 feet
Dam: 126 feet high, 426 feet long, completed - 1913

Though very small in comparison to the other lakes in the chain, Tallulah Lake is quite popular. Situated alongside the newly created Tallulah Gorge State Park, this lake attracts large numbers of bank fishermen and draws scores of swimmers to its sandy white beach. The lake, like its other sisters in the chain, is quite scenic with lovely mountain vistas and numerous cascading streams along its wooded banks.

Tugalo Lake
Surface Area: 597 acres
Shoreline: 18 miles
Elevation: 892 feet
Dam: 155 feet high, 940 feet long, completed - 1923

The last in the chain of lakes within Rabun County, Tugalo is unique in that it has virtually no development and is restricted as to the size of boat motor which may be operated. This is a wilderness lake that attracts mostly fishermen. Make no mistake though, this is a beautiful lake. The Chattooga River flows into the lake from the northeast, and Section IV paddlers are quite familiar with its beautiful wooded shoreline.

The Rabun County Outdoors Companion

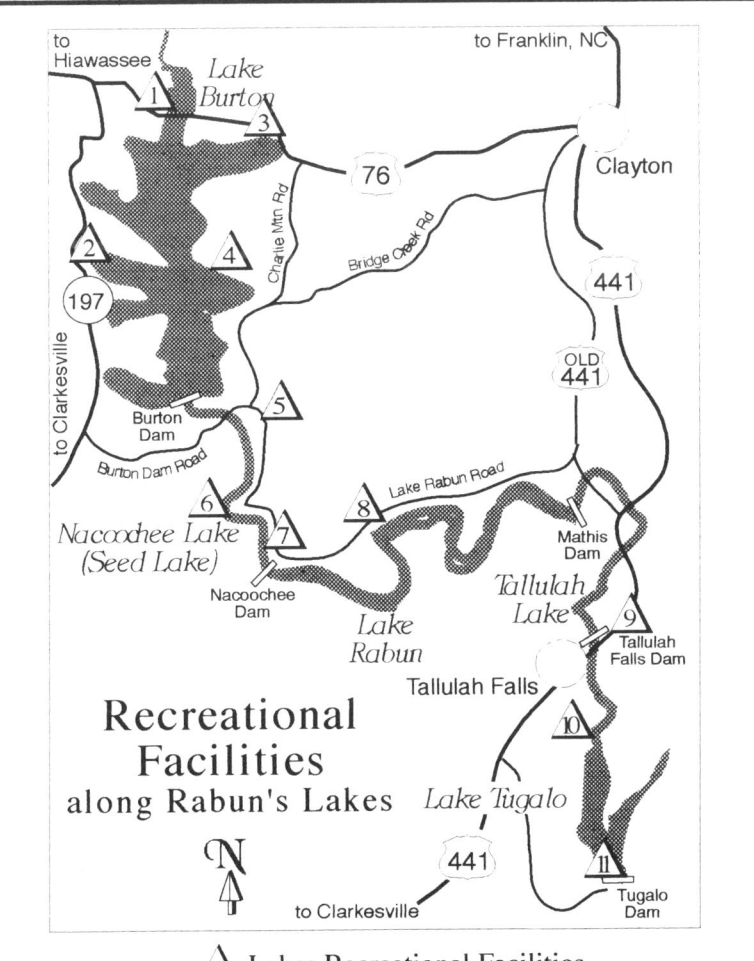

Recreational Facilities along Rabun's Lakes

△ Lakes Recreational Facilities

1 - **Jones Bridge Park** - sheltered picnic facility overlooking lake
2 - **Moccasin Creek State Park**
3 - **Timpson Cove Beach** - beach, picnic area, restrooms
4 - **Murray Cove Boat Launch Area** - paved ramp
5 - **Lake Seed Boat Launch Area** - gravel ramp for small boats
6 - **Lake Seed Campground** - beach, wilderness camping
7 - **Nacoochee Park** - picnic area, restrooms
8 - **Rabun Beach Recreation area** - camping, boat ramps, hiking
9 - **Tallulah Falls State Park**
10 - **Tallulah Point** - sheltered picnic area, restrooms
11 - **Tugalo Park** - Primitive camping, restrooms, boat ramp

The Rabun County Outdoors Companion

Local Boat Rentals, Marinas & Marine Dealers

Anchorage Marina
Hwy 76 West - Lake Burton
Ski and pontoon boat rentals
782-5193 or 782-3013

LaPrade's Marina
Hwy 197 - Lake Burton
Pontoon / fishing boats, canoes
Open seasonally
947-3003

Lakemont Marina
Lake Rabun Road - Lake Rabun
Pontoon boats
782-4981

Mark's Marine
Hwy 76 West - Lake Burton
782-5565

Whitewater Paddling in Rabun County

While nearly everyone is familiar with whitewater boating on the famous Chattooga River, Rabun County has several other options for those wishing to canoe or kayak.

Upper Tallulah River

Length: 4.3 miles to 7 miles
Difficulty: generally easy

This exciting short run begins at the Tallulah River Campground (or other easy access point close by) and provides an enjoyable and highly scenic float down the intimate upper Tallulah. The 4.3 mile section down to the Plum Orchard Road Bridge features several rock laden shoals scattered among the generally calm but always pretty stream. Floaters wishing to continue will encounter the backwaters of Lake Burton at mile 5.0 and come to the US 76 bridge at mile 7. The preferred take-out is about 0.2 mile up Vickers Road from the Hwy 76 bridge. Be careful not to trespass on private property here!

The Rabun County' Outdoors Companion

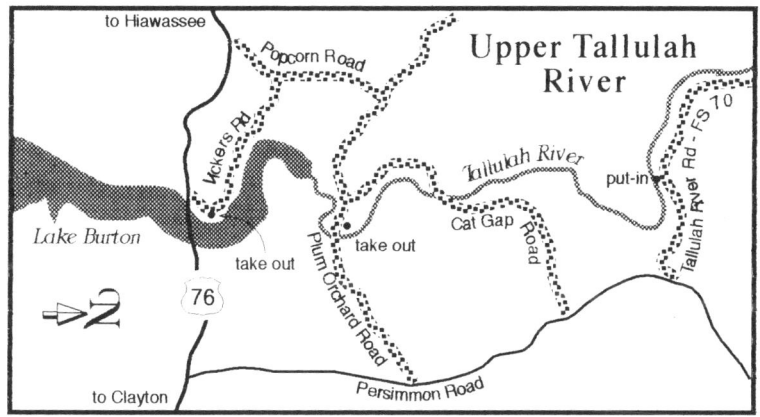

Lower Tallulah River
Length: 5.5 miles
Difficulty: easy to difficult
Hazards: one section of tricky shoals featuring one Class IV ledge.

This particular section of the Tallulah River offers a real variety of floating experiences. The 5.5 miles available to boaters features plenty of calm, placid water, an exciting whitewater stretch and nearly 2 miles of beautiful mountain lake. Almost 4 miles of this trip are situated between Lake Rabun's Mathis Dam and Lake Tallulah along the original riverbed. This portion normally has a reduced flow, as huge tunnels often carry water from Lake Rabun directly to the Terrora generating station just above Lake Tallulah.

The put-in is at the old US 441 bridge near Lakemont, about one mile below Mathis dam. The float for the first few miles is pastoral and calm with the first sizable shoals occuring 2.5 miles into the trip, where several Class II and III shoals spice things up. A bit over 4 miles into this section a prolonged series of challenging ledges occurs just above the Terrora plant. One class IV is particularly tricky and should be run with caution.

Just below the power plant is the backwaters of scenic 63 acre Lake Tallulah. Those wishing to take out may do so at just about any location along old 441 here, including several locations within the Terrora day-use area of Tallulah Falls State Park. Plan to include the lake on your trip, as the scenery along the lake is well worth your effort. See map next page.

The Rabun County Outdoors Companion

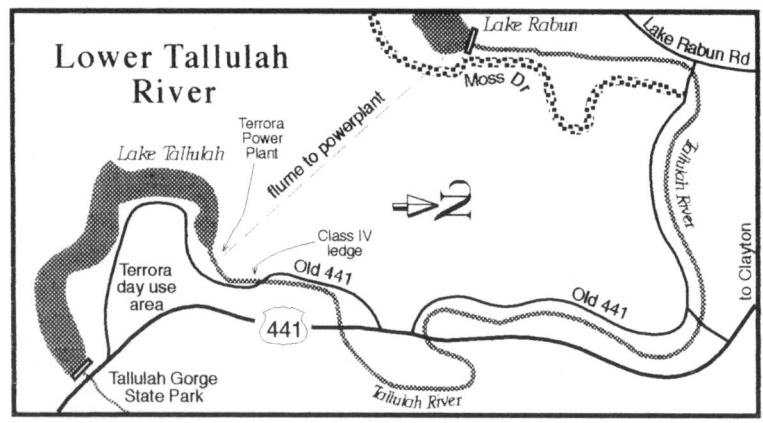

Guided Whitewater Trips & Equipment Rentals

Guided Trips on the Chattooga River

Southeastern Expeditions
Chattooga River Outpost
1 mile west of the Chattooga on Highway 76
Reservations: 1-800-RAFT or (404) 329-0433

Nantahala Outdoor Center
Chattooga River Outpost
4 miles east of Long Creek, SC on SC 37/196 (Chattooga Ridge Rd)
Reservations: (704) 488-6900

Wildwater, Ltd.
Chattooga River Outpost
1 mile north of Long Creek, SC off Highway 76
Reservations: (864) 647-9587

Chattooga Outfitters, Equipment Rentals & Clinics

Chattooga River Adventures
2 miles east of the Chattooga on Highway 76, Long Creek, SC
(864) 647-0365 or 1-(800) UGO-RAFT

Chattooga Whitewater Shop
2.5 miles east of the Chattooga on Highway 76, Long Creek, SC
(864) 647-9083

Horseback Riding

Rocky Gap / Willis Knob Horse Camp & Trails

This excellent system of horse trails features 27.5 miles of magnificent mountain scenery. Located along Section 2 of the Chattooga River, the Rocky Gap/Willis Knob trails cross from Georgia into South Carolina, and include portions of both the Chattahoochee and Sumter National Forests.

Numerous trails offer loops of varying lengths, with three Chattooga River fords providing some added excitement. These fords are normally passable at normal water levels, but the Forest Service recommends the ford at Adline Branch.

On the Georgia side, the Willis Knob Horse Camp is available with reservations. This facility consists of eight sites. Reservations must be made in advance by contacting:

**Tallulah Ranger District
PO Box 438
Clayton, GA 30525
(706) 782-3320**

South Carolina's Whetstone Base Camp can also be reserved in advance. If no reservations have been received, the several sites here are available on a first-come basis. Reservations and additional information may be obtained from:

**Andrew Pickens Ranger District
112 Andrew Pickens Circle
Mountain Rest, SC 29664
(864) 638-9568**

The Forest Service has an informational brochure on the Rocky Gap/Willis Knob Horse trails which includes a diagram of the trails and complete information including reservations and permits. Please contact one of the above agencies for additional information.

Directions: From Clayton, follow Warwoman Road east for 11.6 miles. Turn right onto Goldmine Road (FS 157). Proceed 0.2 mile to the Woodall Ridge Day Use parking area or 1.9 miles

The Rabun County Outdoors Companion

to the Willis Knob Horse Camp.

Smokey Mountain Stables

Smokey Mountain Stables offers pleasant, scenic wooded trails for individuals or groups. Lessons are available by appointment. (706) 782- 5836. Smokey Mountain Stables is located 9 miles south of Clayton (3 miles north of Tallulah Falls) on Highway 441.

Dillard House Stables

Set amidst the beautiful Little Tennessee Valley in Dillard, the Dillard House Stables offer trail rides for all skill levels. Overnight trips and lessons are available. Reservations are highly recommended. (706) 746-2038. Located on the grounds of the Dillard House Restaurant and Inn, Dillard.

Snow Skiing

Sky Valley Resort

As proof that Rabun County is Georgia's most versatile when it comes to recreation, the Sky Valley Resort offers Georgia's only ski operation. Sky Valley offers five ski slopes open anytime from late November to late February - as long as it's cold enough! (706) 746-5302 or 746-5015. Sky Valley Resort is located northeast of Dillard off GA Hwy 246.

Ski Scaly

Although not in Rabun County (or Georgia either for that matter), nearby Ski Scaly offers a popular alternative for skiers. Open generally from late November to late February, weather permitting. To reach Ski Scaly, follow GA Hwy 246 from Dillard. Once across the NC line, the highway becomes NC 106. Continue for several miles to the Scaly community. The ski slope is located adjacent to NC 106.

Trout Fishing

Undoubtedly one of Rabun's most popular outdoor activities is fishing. Hundreds of fishermen enjoy Rabun's incomparable streams, rivers and lakes each year. Fishing on the big lakes - Burton, Seed, Rabun, Tallulah and Tugalo - as mentioned earlier in this section, is quite popular. Yet it is the trout fishing in Rabun's beautiful streams and rivers that attracts the largest number of anglers to the area. Mentioned below are some of the streams open to trout fishing. (Be sure to check the local fishing regulations for any restrictions.)

Chattooga River - Open all year, the upper Chattooga from the Russell Bridge area north to Burrells Ford is very popular with trout fishermen. Access is good via a series of riverside trails. The river here is somewhat large, unlike most of Rabun's fishable streams. Brook, rainbow and brown trout are regularly stocked along this section.

West Fork Chattooga River - A major Chattooga River tributary, the West Fork has been a favorite among trout anglers for years. A sizable stretch of the West Fork runs alongside Hwy 28 from Warwoman Road down to the main Chattooga. Another popular section is found alongside much of Overflow Creek Road (FS 86). Access is mainly through a loose network of riverside trails. Stocked on a regular basis.

Holcomb Creek - a small but significant tributary to the West Fork, portions of Holcomb Creek flow alongside Hale Ridge Road above the FS7/FS 86 intersection.

Tallulah River - Very popular stream in the Coleman River Wildlife Management Area (WMA). The Tallulah River receives very heavy fishing pressure in the prime fishing seasons, and is heavily stocked accordingly. The Tallulah River Road (FS70) parallels the river, offering miles of good access.

Coleman River - Small, generally difficult stream to fish which flows into the Tallulah along FS 70. Fishing with artificial lures only. Stream features wild brook and rainbow trout.

The Rabun County Outdoors Companion

Wildcat Creek - Popular mid-size stream in Lake Burton WMA - easily accessible from Wildcat Creek Road (FS 26). Fairly easy to fish, Wildcat Creek offers browns and rainbows.

Moccasin Creek - Open to children and seniors within Moccasin Creek State Park, this portion of the creek is quite easy to fish. Upstream within the Burton WMA, the small stream is somewhat difficult to fish but offers a fair number of rainbows.

Tuckaluge Creek - Small stream located in the Warwoman WMA which provides moderately easy access via Tuckaluge Road (FS 153). Small native brook trout predominant.

Sarah's Creek - Very popular Warwoman WMA stream. Features easy access along Sarah's Creek Road. Rainbow and brown trout are present, as are usually a lot of other fishermen.

Andy's Trout Farm - Just in case you get skunked, Andy's Trout Farm has several ponds stocked full of trout, just about guaranteeing success. You pay according to what you catch. Pole rentals are available. Normally open April 1 through Thanksgiving. Call (706) 746-2550. From Dillard take Betty's Creek Road for about 5 miles (follow the signs).

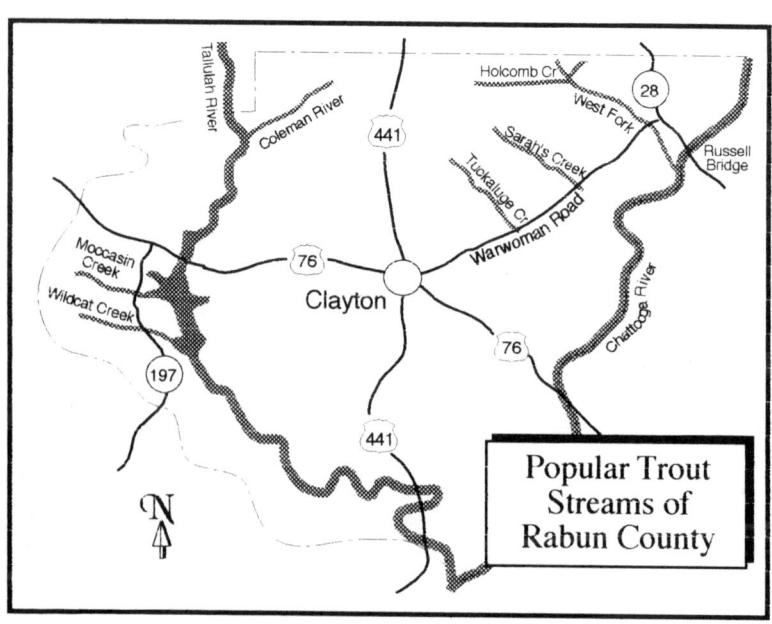

Popular Trout Streams of Rabun County

The Rabun County Outdoors Companion

Campgrounds

Camping remains one of the most popular recreational activities in Rabun County, and the wide variety of settings and facilities is sure to please just about anyone's tastes. Here are just a few of the camping areas in and around Rabun County.

Tallulah River Campground - 17 campsites along upper Tallulah River near Persimmon Road. Located on Tallulah River Road (FS 70).

Sandy Bottoms Campground - 12 campsites along upper Tallulah River near Tate City. Located on Tallulah River Road (FS 70).

Tate Branch Campground - 19 campsites and 10 picnic shelters along upper Tallulah River near Tate City. Located on Tallulah River Road (FS 70).

Rabun Beach Campground - Two camping areas within walking distance of beautiful Lake Rabun. 80 campsites, hiking trails, beach. Located on Lake Rabun Road near Nacoochee Dam.

Overflow Road Campground - Primitive camping area along scenic West Fork Chattooga River. Located on Overflow Creek Road (FS 86) near Warwoman Road.

Moccasin Creek State Park - Shady campground on scenic Lake Burton. 53 campsites, boat ramp, fishing, picnic area. Moccasin Creek is located on Hwy 197 on Lake Burton's western shoreline.

Black Rock Mountain State Park - Georgia's highest park offers 53 tent and trailer sites, 11 walk-in sites, 2 picnic shelters, fishing, hiking and plenty of scenery. Black Rock Mountain State Park is located just west of Mountain City.

Tallulah Gorge State Park - Our newest state park offers 50 tent and trailer sites, tennis, swimming, hiking, fishing and picnicing. Tallulah Gorge State Park is located in Tallulah Falls along Hwy 441.

The Rabun County Outdoors Companion

Call the US Forest Service at (706) 782-3320 to inquire about reservations at Forest Service campgrounds. Call the state parks directly to check on campsite availability. See Section 1 for appropriate numbers.

Several other private campgrounds and RV parks are available locally. Call for additional details and availability.

Appalachian Camper Park - Hwy 441 North near Tallulah Falls. (706) 754-9319.

Christian's Warwoman Campground - Warwoman Road near Warwoman Dell Recreation Area. (706) 782-6810.

Mountain City RV Park - located on Hwy 441 in Mountain City. (706) 746-6985.

Golf

Sky Valley Resort -18 hole golf course, driving range and pro shop. (706) 746-5303. Located in Sky Valley Resort.

Rabun County Golf Club - 9 hole public course. (706) 782-5500. Located on Old Hwy 441 about 2 miles south of Clayton.

Rabun County Park

Rabun County Park features a wide variety of recreational facilities for the enjoyment of visitors and residents alike. Among the activities featured here - softball, baseball, basketball, volleyball, soccer, aerobics and swimming. The park also features a horse ring, pavilion, picnic sites and pond.

The Rabun County Recreation Department offers an excellent choice of programs and activites. Call (706) 782-4600 for additional details.

Ellicott Rock Wilderness

Although only a relatively small portion lies within Rabun County, beautiful and unspoiled Ellicott Rock Wilderness is an excellent destination for anyone interested in exploring this area. This 9,000+ acre area, first established over 30 years ago, encompasses a greatly diverse region where North Carolina, Georgia and South Carolina meet. If you want to explore Ellicott Rock Wilderness, it will have to be on foot. No horses, mountain bikes or ORVs are permitted.

The incomparable upper Chattooga bisects the heart of the wilderness, and several excellent trails traverse across ridges, up mountain peaks and across rushing streams. There is good news and bad news here, though. The bad news is that none of these paths explore the Rabun portion of the wilderness. The good news is that all of the trails are easy to reach and within short driving distance of northeast Rabun County.

Check with the Forest Service office in Clayton for maps and other publications dealing with this magnificent wilderness area. Ellicott Rock Wilderness is a fantastic destination for hikers, campers, fishermen and outdoor lovers of all types.

Ellicott Rock Wilderness can be accessed from Burrells Ford or the Walhalla Fish Hatchery off Hwy 107 in South Carolina, or from Bull Pen Road (also off Hwy 107) in North Carolina. See map on page vii for general location.

The Rabun County Outdoors Companion

Sightseeing by Automobile

One of the easiest and most enjoyable ways to experience the beauty of Rabun County is from the comfort of your automobile. Pick up a local map and plan your own driving tour, or try one of the routes suggested below. All mileages given are very general, due to all the variables involved in driving. All of these trips would generally take 1-2 hours driving time.

Lakes Tour - This drive features lake vistas, scenic mountain overlooks and plenty of side attractions.

From Clayton, follow old Highway 441 south for about 8 miles to Lake Rabun Road on the right. Follow this highly scenic winding road along beautiful Lake Rabun. Continue until the road passes Rabun Beach Recreation Area. Moments afterwards you will pass the Nacoochee Dam and park.

Continue on along the Seed Lake shoreline. The road soon crosses the Tallulah River just below Burton Dam and proceeds up to an intersection with Hwy 197. Turn right and proceed about 8 miles up the west side of Lake Burton. Of special note on this stretch is LaPrade's Fish Camp & Marina and Moccasin Creek State Park. Follow Hwy 197 up to its junction with Hwy 76. Go left and you will follow a high ridgeline for several miles out to Dick's Creek Gap and the Appalachian Trail crossing. The Popcorn Overlook is also a popular stop, providing excellent vistas to the north.

Turn around and proceed east on Hwy 76 back past Hwy 197 and across the upper arm of Lake Burton. Proceed another 12 miles back to Clayton. Be sure to take a map with you, as you may wish to explore some of the dozens of side roads in the area.

Chattooga/Warwoman Loop - Features scenic Chattooga River and plenty of mountain vistas.

Take US 76 east from Clayton. Pass over the Chattooga River and into South Carolina about nine miles southeast of Clayton. Proceed several miles up the long hill and turn left onto Chattooga Ridge Road at the Chattooga River Adventures establishment. Follow this long, winding road through the 4-way stop at Whetstone Road and up to the stop sign at Hwy 28 near Mountain Rest.

Turn left here and follow Hwy 28 up through Callas Gap and

descend back down into the Long Bottom Ford area of the Chattooga River. Proceed across Russell Bridge back into Georgia. Several miles past the bridge, look for Warwoman Road on the left. Proceed 14 miles back to Clayton.

Patterson Gap / Betty's Creek Loop - Features beautiful mountain valleys, forested coves and splashing creeks.

From Clayton, take Hwy 76 west for 8 miles, then bear right onto Persimmon Road. Follow Persimmon north for just over 5 miles. The road then becomes gravel - Patterson Gap Road (FS 32) and traverses an open valley before passing the Tumbling Waters Camp for Girls before ascending up to Patterson Gap along the narrow, twisting route.

Continue past the gap and descend down through Moon Valley and intersect Betty's Creek Road. Turn left here to drive several miles up to Andy's Trout Farm or go right and out to Hwy 441 in Dillard. Turn right onto Hwy 441 to return to Clayton.

Upper Tallulah / Tate City - Features spectacular upper gorge of the Tallulah River and excellent mountain vistas.

From Clayton, take Hwy 76 west for 8 miles, then bear right onto Persimmon Road. Follow Persimmon north for 4 miles. Turn left onto Tallulah River Road (FS 70) and proceed 9 miles up the rugged, one lane road alongside the highly scenic Tallulah River. The beautiful valley known as Tate City is about 6 miles up the road and features sweeping views of the surrounding mountains. The road deadends several miles across the North Carolina line. Note: this road is quite narrow and winding and carries a fair amount of traffic - use caution.

The Rabun County Outdoors Companion

Emergency Information

POLICE

Clayton	782-3333
Mountain City	746-2621
Mountain Patrol (lakes)	782-5807
Rabun County Sheriff	782-3612
Highway Patrol	1-706-886-4949

AMBULANCE

Rabun County EMS	782-7777
Rabun County Rescue Squad	782-3334

FIRE DEPARMENT

Clayton	782-3334
Sky Valley	1-704-526-4131
Forest Fires	782-3320

The Rabun County Outdoors Companion

The Rabun County Outdoors Companion

Other publications from...

FERN CREEK PRESS

The Chattooga Wild and Scenic River, 3rd edition. Excellent all-around guide to whitewater adventure, hiking and camping on the incomparable Chattooga River. 124 pgs. Maps, photos. $9.95.

Waterfalls of the Southern Appalachians, 3rd edition. Guide to over 150 magnificent mountain cascades. Over 25,000 sold! 160 pgs. Complete directions, maps and photos. $9.95 ppd.

The Highlands-Cashiers Outdoors Companion, features over 30 natural attractions in the scenic Highlands, NC area. A favorite! Newly revised, 80 pgs. Complete maps and photos. $7.95.

The Rabun County Outdoors Companion, voted one of the 100 most beautiful counties in America by *Outside* magazine, come explore the mountains, rivers and streams of this scenic area. Contains recreational information of all kinds. 112 pgs. Complete maps and photos. $7.95.

The Tallulah Falls Railroad - A Photographic Remembrance, A collection of photographic images detailing the famous Tallulah Falls shortline, which ran from 1898 to 1961. Over 125 photos. 64 pgs. 8.5" x 11". $11.95.

Yesterday's Rabun, A look back at the history of scenic Rabun County as told by over 170 classic photographic images. 116 pages. $11.95.

Biking the Trails of Rabun, A collection of 30 exciting biking trips in beautiful Rabun County. Also features a great deal of general information on mountain biking, equipment, etc. 190 pgs. Complete maps and photos. 8.5" x 5.5". $9.95.

coming in June 1999!
100 Great Destinations in the North Georgia Mountains...

to receive any of these publications, send check or money order along with $1.00 shipping (GA residents add 7% sales tax) to:

Fern Creek Press
PO Box 1322
Clayton, GA 30525

for additional information, visit our website at: www.rabun.net/boyd

The Rabun County Outdoors Companion

Clayton Photo

One hour Film Processing (C-41 color print film)

Film - A large assortment of film and video tapes from Kodak, Fuji, Ilford, Polaroid and more.

Cameras - From single use to the best in point and shoot, to SLR's including Minolta, Kodak and Olympus.

Accessories, Frames, Gifts, Postcards & More!

A full service Photo & Imaging Center

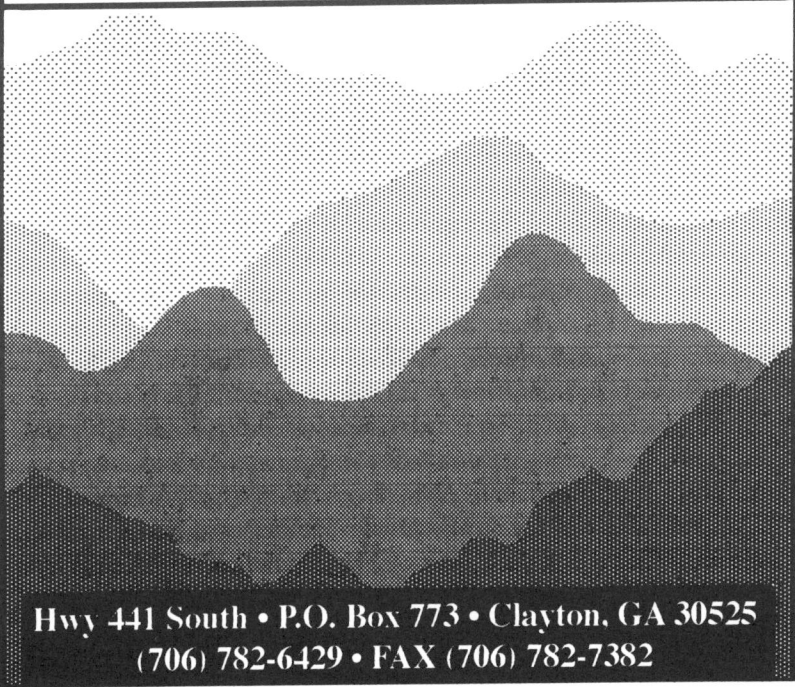

Hwy 441 South • P.O. Box 773 • Clayton, GA 30525
(706) 782-6429 • FAX (706) 782-7382

The Rabun County Outdoors Companion

Allen's Books 'N Crafts

GENERAL BOOK STORE
BEST SELLERS & NEW RELEASES
REFERENCE MATERIAL & SPECIAL ORDER

Music - Compact Discs & Cassettes

Genealogical Forms
Collectors Plates

782-7190
DEPOT CENTER
HWY 441 • CLAYTON, GA

THE YORK HOUSE

HISTORIC COUNTRY INN

Real Historic Charm !

Experience romance, relaxation & unsurpassed hospitality at Georgia's oldest Bed & Breakfast Inn. All rooms have period antiques & private baths. Come rock on our 100 year old verandahs !

For reservations call 706-746-2068 or 800-231-YORK
In Mountain City, GA, between Clayton & Dillard, a quarter mile off Hwy. 441

The Rabun County Outdoors Companion
The Wild And Scenic Chattooga River

CLAYTON, GA. Southeastern Expeditions is your full service Chattooga outfitter. We specialize in wilderness outings that can include day and overnight river trips, (raft, canoe or kayak); hikes and hiker shuttle service; and team building workshops. We also arrange lodging and dining at select area properties, group cook-outs and camp-outs. For local weather conditions, and hiking information call 706-782-4331. **To reserve your adventure and for a FREE color brochure, call 1-800-868-7238.**

Established in 1973, Southeastern Expeditions operates under a permit from the U.S. Forest Service.

The Rabun County Outdoors Companion

Glen Ella Springs Inn

*T*he road to our front door is unpaved...
that's how our guests like it.

Off the beaten path in the Northeast Georgia Mountains, near some of the area's best hiking and biking trails, a warm, rustic, but classy 100-year-old inn with cozy fireplaces, lovely views, genuine hospitality and outstanding food. Come for dinner, a romantic weekend or an executive retreat.

Route 3, Bear Gap Road Clarkesville, GA 30523

Please call for reservations:
(706) 754-7295

New Cabins • Secluded and Surrounded by
Deep Forests • Fireplaces • Grills • Porches to
Enjoy the Beauty of Nature

706-782-7542

Route 1, Box 2173
Boggs Mountain Church Rd • Tiger, GA 30576

Conveniently located 2 miles off Hwy 441
3 miles south of Clayton

The Rabun County Outdoors Companion

the Stockton House RESTAURANT

706-782-6175

Open Daily • All Year
Lunch & Dinner

Closed:
Easter Sunday
2nd Monday in June
Christmas Day

One Mile East of Clayton on Warwoman Road

LUNCH BUFFET • SANDWICHES • STEAKS • SEAFOOD

THE STOCKTON HOUSE RESTAURANT, Warwoman Road, Clayton, is located on a rise above Warwoman Valley, with an excellent view of Screamer Mountain. Its light airy atmosphere adds to the charm of the tasty fare served for lunch and dinner.

WE APPRECIATE YOUR BUSINESS

Co-Op Crafts

- Wood Toys
- Jams & Jellies
- Local Books

- Locally Made Crafts
- Quilts
- Pottery

2 Great Locations -
**Tallulah Falls - Old Train Depot • 754-6810
Dillard - Hwy 441 • 746-5990**

The Rabun County Outdoors Companion

800-UGO RAFT
CHATTOOGA RIVER ADVENTURES

RAFT RENTALS
Custom Guided Lake Canoe & Kayak Tours

- Clinics • Outfitters Shop
- Whitewater Equipment Sales
- Backpacking/Camping Supplies
- Video
- Photography
- Lodging Available

1-864-647-0365

Two miles from Chattooga River Bridge - Highway 76 in South Carolina
14546-B Long Creek Hwy., Mtn. Rest, SC 29664

English Manor Inns
BED AND BREAKFAST

Romantic Getaways • Family Refreshers
Guest Rooms & Private Jacuzzi Suites
Groups • Conferences

1-800-782-5780

HWY 76 EAST • CLAYTON, GEORGIA 30525

The Rabun County Outdoors Companion

Notes

About the Author & Fern Creek Press

Brian Boyd, a native of Stone Mountain, Georgia, is a lifelong resident of North Georgia. He and his family have resided in beautiful Rabun County since 1991. Brian has a degree in journalism from the University of Georgia and founded Fern Creek Press in 1989. Brian created Fern Creek Press to provide easy-to-use guidebooks and maps for the many visitors who wish to explore this magnificent region.

To date, Brian and Fern Creek Press have published nine books, including *The Chattooga Wild and Scenic River*, *Summits of the South*, *The Highlands-Cashiers Outdoors Companion* and the ever-popular *Waterfalls of the Southern Appalachians*, now in its third edition.

Brian is an avid outdoorsman, and has written for several magazines and publications over the last 10 years. In addition to writing, he enjoys hiking (obviously), whitewater canoeing, tennis, photography, gardening and even yardwork.

Future plans for Fern Creek Press include publishing a "best-of" guide to the Northeast Georgia mountains, a "Senior Citizens" guidebook to the region and numerous other maps, posters and postcards. Additionally, Brian offers consultations on trips into the region and offers personally led hikes to interested parties. Call (706) 782-5379 for details.